FROM MANY CULTURES,
One HISTORY

Triumphs and Struggles
for
LATINO CIVIL RIGHTS

Bárbara C. Cruz

Enslow Publishers, Inc.
40 Industrial Road
Box 398
Berkeley Heights, NJ 07922
USA
        http://www.enslow.com

For the girls: Cristina & Amanda Yelvington, Raquel & Patricia Farinas, and Nadia Acosta. And for Dr. Rosa Castro Feinberg, who has dedicated her life to the struggle.

Library of Congress Cataloging-in-Publication Data

Cruz, Bárbara.
    Triumphs and struggles for Latino civil rights / Bárbara C. Cruz.
      p. cm. — (From many cultures, one history)
      Includes bibliographical references and index.
    Audience: Grades 4-6.
    ISBN-13: 978-0-7660-2804-3
    ISBN-10: 0-7660-2804-6
      1. Hispanic Americans—Civil rights—History—Juvenile literature.
    2. Immigrants—Civil rights—United States—History—Juvenile literature.
    3. Civil rights movements—United States—History—Juvenile literature.
    4. Hispanic Americans—Social conditions—Juvenile literature.
    5. Hispanic Americans—Economic conditions—Juvenile literature.
    6. United States—Ethnic relations—Juvenile literature. I. Title.
    E184.S75C775 2008
    323.119468073—dc22

                            2007020276

Printed in the United States of America

10 9 8 7 6 5 4 3 2 1

Illustration Credits: Associated Press, pp. 10, 15, 28, 36, 42, 54, 64, 70, 73, 78, 89, 93, 96, 97, 106, 110; César Chávez Foundation, p. 32; Denver Public Library, Colorado Historical Society, and Denver Art Museum, p. 83; Enslow Publishers, Inc., pp. 13, 20; Courtesy of Gary Soto, p. 99; JFK Library, p. 39; Library of Congress, p. 4; NASA photo, pp. 102, 116 (right); North Wind Picture Archives, p. 22; Oregon State University Archives, pp. 85, 115; Serra International, p. 19; U.S. Department of Defense, p. 104; Walter P. Reuther Library, Wayne State University, pp. 6, 8, 116 (left).

Cover Illustration: Associated Press/Ron Haviv/VII.

Contents

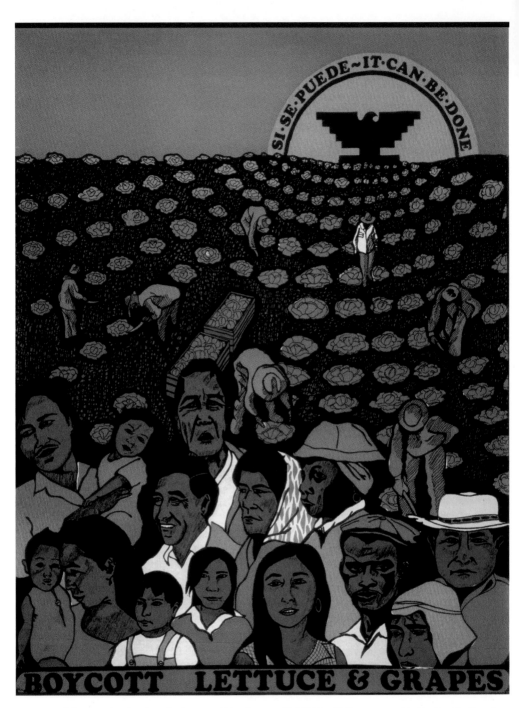

César Chávez's United Farm Workers (UFW) did not end their fight for rights in the 1960s. This 1978 UFW poster promotes a boycott of lettuce and grapes.

CHAPTER One

Fighting for Rights

César Chávez knew firsthand how hard life could be as a migrant farmworker. His own family had lost their farm in Arizona during the Great Depression, and they were forced to look for work as migrant farmers. It was 1966, and most farmworkers lived in the cramped quarters of labor camps, often ten or more people in a trailer home. Usually their housing had no bathrooms, no electricity, and no running water.

Chávez had founded the National Farm Workers Association (NFWA) to help improve conditions for farmworkers. In 1965, Chávez had joined a strike and boycott of table grapes initiated by the Filipino grape workers who were members of the Agricultural Workers Organizing Committee (AWOC). A year later, the farm owners still had not made enough

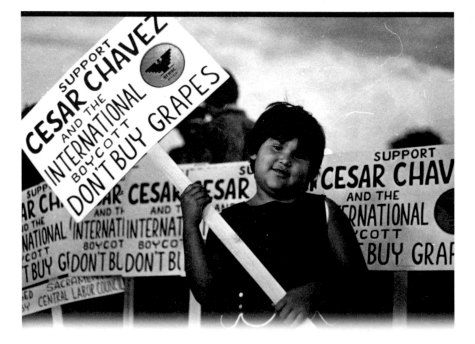

A child carries a sign supporting the international boycott of grapes.

changes to improve the workers' dismal conditions. Chávez knew something dramatic needed to be done to call attention to the farmworkers' struggle.

In the winter of 1966, Chávez and NFWA began with AWOC to organize a 340-mile march from Delano, where he lived, to the California capital, Sacramento. He hoped that the march would bring even more attention to the strike and would also recruit new union members. He planned the march to begin on March 17 and end on Easter Sunday.

Because it would be during the Lenten season, Chávez called it a *peregrinación*, or pilgrimage. A pilgrimage is a long journey usually taken for a moral or spiritual purpose. Lent refers to the forty-day period before Easter in Christianity. It is a holy time marked by fasting and personal sacrifice.

As the procession worked its way through the small towns, hundreds of people greeted the marchers and sometimes joined them, helping them carry the flags to the next town. The march eventually took twenty-five grueling days.

After just the first day, painful blisters covered the marchers' feet. One marcher said, "Some people had bloody feet. Some would keep on walking and you'd see blood coming out of their shoes."[1] One of Chávez's legs swelled, and he developed a high fever. Despite the severe pain and the fever, Chávez refused medication and continued on the march, using a cane to help him walk.

Each night when the marchers stopped, they held a meeting to rally support and to educate the public. Hundreds of families hosted the marchers in each town, offering them a meal, a shower, and a bed to rest in preparation for the next day's walk.

When the march ended on Easter Sunday as planned, about ten thousand people joined Chávez and the marchers on the steps of the capitol. Dr. Martin Luther King, Jr. sent Chávez a telegram. In it, Dr. King sent his best wishes to Chávez and

César Chávez (left) walks with a cane during the 340-mile march in 1966 meant to bring attention to the farm-worker strike.

the UFW: "Our separate struggles are really one—a struggle for freedom, for dignity, and for humanity . . . We are together with you in spirit and in determination that our dreams for a better tomorrow will be realized."[2] Like African Americans, Mexican Americans have had to work hard to ensure that their rights are respected and protected.

César Chávez

César Chávez was born on March 31, 1927, near Yuma, Arizona. Although the Chávez family was far from rich, they led a comfortable life with everyone in the family helping in the family business (a combination grocery store, garage, and pool hall).

Then, in 1929, the Great Depression changed the family's life forever. Just like millions of other Americans who lost their jobs and homes, the Chávez family was forced to sell their business. Like thousands of others, the family left their home and moved to California in search of jobs. César's family became migrant farmworkers.

As his parents followed the harvest of different fruits and vegetables, César and his siblings helped pick crops and went to school when they could. César and his family sometimes lived in migrant worker camps. Other times, they had no choice but to camp out under bridges and in shacks made out of cardboard and tar paper.

These painful memories would serve Chávez well. Knowing from firsthand experience how hard life could be as a farm laborer, Chávez went on to create the UFW shortly after his famous march in 1966. Today the UFW continues its work to protect and represent farmworkers throughout the United States.

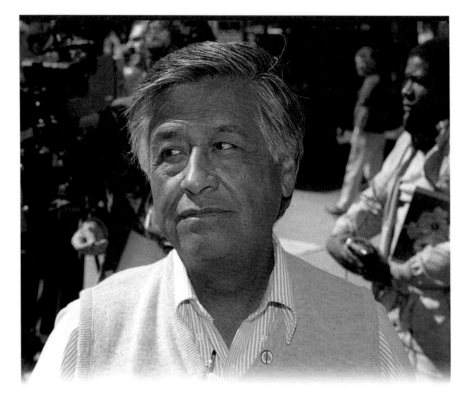

César Chávez is pictured on June 29, 1989, about a year after he fasted for twenty-five days in protest of the dangers of pesticides to farm workers and their families.

Chávez and his associates continued to work tirelessly to improve the lives of farmworkers, bringing awareness of their terrible conditions to the U.S. public. Those Americans who supported the UFW responded by not buying table grapes. By 1969, almost three quarters of the California grape growers were out of business. By the spring of 1970, an agreement between the remaining growers and the union was finally signed. No one could believe that ordinary citizens had triumphed over the rich and powerful growers. Chávez was especially pleased when, in 1975, California passed the Agricultural Labor Relations Act, which recognized the rights of farmworkers to organize and bargain collectively.

Chávez's determined struggle for justice is but one story among many in the history of Latinos in the United States. And the struggle for justice and equality continues today.

Who Are the Latinos?

The terms *Hispanic* and *Latino* are used more or less interchangeably in the United States. However, for some people the use of the terms is controversial. The federal government commonly uses "Hispanic," but many argue that the term tends to stress European (Spanish) roots. Some people favor "Latino" because it puts more emphasis on Latin-American origins. Furthermore, many Latinos emphasize their "mixed" heritage—that of Europeans, native peoples, and Africans.

Latinos are not one culture or one nationality. They are people whose families have origins in South America, Central America, Mexico, or the Spanish-speaking Caribbean. Today, about 13 percent of the U.S. population is made up of Latinos.[1] The states with the largest concentrations of Latinos are

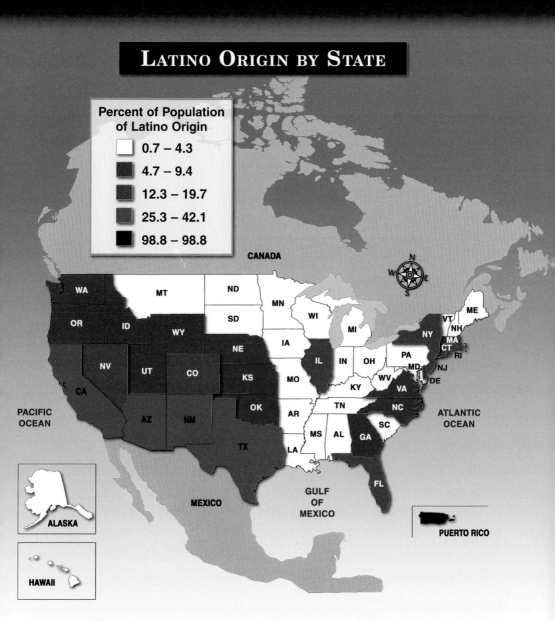

LATINO ORIGIN BY STATE

Percent of Population of Latino Origin

- 0.7 – 4.3
- 4.7 – 9.4
- 12.3 – 19.7
- 25.3 – 42.1
- 98.8 – 98.8

CANADA

WA, MT, ND, MN, WI, MI, ME, VT, NH, NY, MA, CT, RI, OR, ID, WY, IA, PA, MD, NJ, NV, UT, CO, NE, IL, IN, OH, WV, DE, CA, KS, MO, KY, VA, AZ, NM, OK, AR, TN, NC, SC, TX, LA, MS, AL, GA, FL

PACIFIC OCEAN

ATLANTIC OCEAN

MEXICO

GULF OF MEXICO

ALASKA

HAWAII

PUERTO RICO

Puerto Rico, a commonwealth of the United States, has the highest percentage of people of Hispanic or Latino origin. The states with the highest percentages are California, Arizona, New Mexico, and Texas. All of these states share a border with Mexico.

I am Joaquín
Yo Soy Joaquín

Rodolfo "Corky" Gonzales published his poem *Yo Soy Joaquín (I Am Joaquín)* in 1967. In it, Gonzales shared his new cosmological idea of the "Chicano," a person who is neither Indian nor European, neither Mexican nor American, but a mixture of many identities. It encourages Chicano youths to find pride in their culture and history.

Juan Felipe Herrera, a professor at the University of California at Riverside, remembered that when the poem was published, it caused a sensation throughout the Latino community. Herrera says, "Here, finally, was our collective song, and it arrived like thunder crashing down from the heavens. Every little barrio newspaper from Albuquerque to Berkeley published it. People slapped mimeographed copies up on walls and telephone poles."[2]

California, Colorado, Arizona, New Mexico, Texas, Florida, Illinois, New York, and New Jersey.

Latinos go by different names. Some prefer to just use the term *Hispanic* or *Latino*. Many others refer to the specific country of origin, for example, Colombian American, Cuban American, or Mexican American. Many Mexican Americans prefer the term

The Folklorico dance troupe takes part in the Piñatafest parade in Roswell, New Mexico, in 2003. The annual festival celebrates Latino culture.

Chicano, an identification that has political implications and reflects ethnic pride. Some Puerto Ricans called themselves *Boriqua* or even *Nuyorican* if they are from New York.

There are at least two ways to identify Latinos. There are those whose ancestors have been in the United States for generations but still retain the culture and/or language. There are also recent immigrants from Spanish-speaking countries who are also considered Latino. The U.S. Census Bureau defines Hispanic citizens as "those who indicated that their origin was Mexican, Puerto Rican, Cuban, Central or South American, or some other Hispanic origin."[3] As of 2007, there were over 42 million Latinos, the largest ethnic minority in the United States.[4]

While they seem to be one of the latest immigrant groups to enter the United States, Latinos have been a vital force in the nation's history since before the people from England settled in Jamestown, Virginia, in 1607.

CHAPTER Three

Coming to America

Many are surprised to learn that Spanish-speaking people were living in what is now known as the United States over fifty years before English colonists settled in Jamestown, Virginia. When Christopher Columbus sailed to the Americas, he sailed under the Spanish flag for King Ferdinand and Queen Isabella. Many other Spanish explorers were sent in the years that followed to find gold and other riches. As land was claimed, the Spanish empire grew in the Americas so that eventually it included much of the present-day United States, Mexico, and most of Central and South America.

The oldest city on the U.S. mainland is St. Augustine, Florida, established by Spanish soldiers in 1565. Spanish explorer Juan Ponce de León claimed the area in 1513, looking for gold, silver, and other treasures. The Spanish had claimed San Juan, Puerto Rico, two years earlier. In addition to the riches they were seeking, the Spanish also sent Catholic priests to protect the explorers and to spread the word of Christianity. These friars, also called missionaries, often converted the native people to Catholicism. Some of these priests established missions—religious outposts that often became the heart of new communities.

One of the most well-known missionaries was Father Junípero Serra, a Franciscan priest. In 1769, he founded a mission in California in the San Diego area. Eventually, twenty-one missions were established throughout what is now the state of California, from San Francisco in the north to San Diego in the south. The Spanish founded other missions in the Southwest including New Mexico, Arizona, and Texas.

As the colonists sought independence from Great Britain, the Hispanic presence continued to grow. As the American patriots rebelled against English rule, many Hispanics outside the British colonies aligned themselves with the revolutionaries. Bernardo de Gálvez, governor of Louisiana, helped George Washington and his men during the American Revolution. He aided the Americans in their fight against the British by allowing badly needed supplies to be shipped up the Mississippi

River to patriot forces in the north. Later Gálvez commanded troops in battle against the British. In Cuba, the "Havana Ladies" donated their jewelry and diamonds to finance the battle of Yorktown.[1] *Las Damas de la Havana* were able to raise over one million pounds sterling.

Once the new nation was established, people started moving west as the U.S. government gave more and more incentives for settling. As people moved into areas that had been originally inhabited by Americans Indians and Spanish-speaking people, clashes inevitably ensued.

In 1836, Texas (still a possession of Mexico) declared itself independent. The disagreement marks the beginning of the Mexican-American War. The Mexican-American War ended with the signing of the Treaty of Guadalupe Hidalgo in 1848. Through this agreement, the United States gained not only Texas but also New Mexico, California, and parts of several

Father Junípero Serra helped spread Spanish culture to California in the eighteenth century.

other states. As a result, Mexico lost half its national territory.

Instantaneously, about seventy-eight thousand residents of these lands became U.S. citizens. Just a few years later, in 1853, Mexico sold land to the U.S. by means of the Gadsden Purchase. This treaty covered 30,000 square miles of land that included parts of Arizona and New Mexico, south of the Gila River. All of this land amounted to what some Mexican Americans later called "The Lost Land."

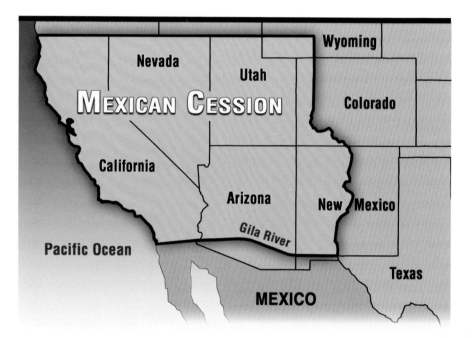

After Mexico ceded land to the United States under the Treaty of Guadalupe Hidalgo, a large number of Mexicans suddenly found themselves living in the United States. The land became all or part of seven present-day states.

During the U.S. Civil War, Hispanics also left their mark on U.S. history. About ten thousand Hispanics fought in the conflict, serving in both the Confederacy and the Union. Two Hispanic Union Navy servicemen, Philip Bazaar and John Ortega, won the Congressional Medal of Honor. Cuban-American Loreta Janeta Velázquez disguised herself as a man to fight for the Confederacy. Only after she was injured in battle was her identity revealed. David G. Farragut, son of Spanish immigrant Jorge Farragut, was the Navy's first four-star admiral. In the Civil War's Battle of New Orleans, he gave his famous order, "Damn the torpedoes! Full steam ahead!"

As the United States was battling its own bloody civil war, in the Caribbean, Cuba and Puerto Rico began fighting for their independence from Spain. After the U.S.S. *Maine* was blown up in Havana Harbor in 1898, the United States entered the war against Spain. After five months of fighting, the Spanish-American War was brought to a close in 1898. In a treaty signed between Spain and the United States, Cuba was freed from Spanish control. Spain also gave the territories of Puerto Rico, Guam, and the Philippines to the United States. Cuba and the Philippines eventually became independent nations, but Puerto Rico and Guam became "possessions" of the United States.

American troops enter San Juan, Puerto Rico, during the 1898 Spanish-American War.

The U.S. Congress passed the Platt Amendment in 1902. Under this law the United States could intervene in Cuban matters at any time. Presumably, this was to maintain Cuba's independence and stability. But critics argued that Cuba was free in name only; the United States *really* controlled the island nation.

In 1917, the Jones Act granted all Puerto Ricans U.S. citizenship. The act did not allow Puerto Ricans to vote in national elections but it did make them eligible for the military draft. While many welcomed the new status, many native Puerto Ricans protested the act, saying that it was just a ploy to increase the pool of eligible draftees for World War I. Many also believed that it would keep Puerto Rico from ever becoming independent.

Right after World War I, South Americans started coming to the United States in large numbers. Many of the new immigrants settled in the Jackson Heights neighborhood in New York City. Even today, it is the largest South American community in the United States. People from places such as Ecuador, Peru, and Colombia have created a vibrant community.

In 1929, when the stock market crashed and heralded the beginning of the Great Depression, Latinos were especially hard hit. As people lost their jobs and homes, the government began to repatriate, or return, as many immigrants as possible to their homeland to free up resources. In particular, about

The Case of Private Félix Longoria

Despite their service, Latinos were not always treated equally in the military. One case that made this unequal treatment painfully real was the case of Private Félix Longoria. In 1948, the body of Private Longoria, who was a Mexican American, was recovered from the Philippines. Private Longoria had been killed on a mission and his remains were sent home for burial with honors.

In Longoria's hometown of Three Rivers, Texas, the cemetery was separated into two sections: one for Mexicans and one for Anglos. Barbed wire separated the two. The director of the town's only funeral home refused to allow the Longoria family to use the chapel.

With the help of Dr. Héctor García, a war veteran who had created an organization to provide Latino veterans with adequate health care, Longoria's widow contacted the press and Texas congressmen to seek their support. Lyndon B. Johnson, then a senator, arranged for a burial at Arlington National Cemetery. Finally, on February 16, 1949, the Longoria family, accompanied by Senator Johnson, was able to bury Private Longoria with full military honors. While the delay of the burial was a tragic reminder of the discrimination that existed in the country, it was also encouraging that the U.S. government was paying attention to Hispanics' struggle for civil rights.[2]

one million Mexican immigrants left the United States and returned to Mexico.

The 1930s saw a steady influx of Puerto Ricans to New York City. Many of them settled into a neighborhood that eventually was called Spanish Harlem or, simply, *El Barrio* (the neighborhood). After World War II, the flow from Puerto Rico to the United States (especially New York City) increased greatly. Today there are more Puerto Ricans living in New York than in San Juan, the capital of Puerto Rico.

In 1959 Fidel Castro, Ernesto "Che" Guevara, and their associates overthrew the government of Fulgencio Batista in Cuba. When Castro officially became the prime minister, he suspended the Constitution and assumed total power. Castro and his government took over private businesses and made them public property. Opponents to his government were imprisoned or executed. The United States' initial fear that Castro would turn the country toward communism was realized when Cuba aligned itself with the Soviet Union.

Thousands of Cubans fled the island and settled in the United States, primarily in Miami, Florida, in an area that became known as "Little Havana." Many of the Cuban refugees planned to return home once the revolution subsided. However, that did not occur. With the realization that they would never be able to return to their homeland, they began making the United States their permanent home.

Operation Pedro Pan
December 26, 1960–October 23, 1962

Soon after Fidel Castro's revolution in Cuba, rumors spread throughout the island that the new socialist government would take children away from their parents and send them to schools and work camps in the Soviet Union.

With the help of the Catholic Church, frightened families began sending their children alone to Miami in a program that became known as Operación Pedro Pan (Operation Peter Pan). Supported by the U.S. government, more than fourteen thousand Cuban children arrived in the United States. About half went to live with family members already in the United States. The rest were placed with host American families and orphanages in thirty states that volunteered to take in the children.[3]

While most families assumed they would soon be reunited, the Cuban Missile Crisis of 1962 disrupted unification efforts and some of the children remained separated from their families for years.

Despite the challenges faced by the Pedro Pan children, they have enjoyed great success in their new homeland, becoming professionals such as teachers, doctors, and journalists.[4] Some of the more well-known Pedro Pan children include Willy Chirino, popular salsa musician; U.S. Senator Mel Martinez; and artist Ana Mendieta.

Cuban immigrants slowly trickled into the United States in the years that followed the Cuban Revolution. But in 1980, a large group of about 125,000 refugees arrived from the port of Mariel. Known as *Marielitos*, their arrival at first led to anti-immigrant feelings. Eventually, the Marielitos found a way to become part of American society.

Dominicans also form a large part of the Latino population in the United States. The tangled history of the Dominican Republic and the United States goes back to at least 1916, when political and economic turmoil prompted the United States to occupy the island. With a military government in place, the occupation ended in 1924, when a new government was democratically elected.

The peace was short lived, however. In 1930, military leader Rafael L. Trujillo took over the government. While Trujillo promoted some economic development, he was known for brutally repressing human rights. He stayed in power until 1961, when he was assassinated.

Trujillo's assassination led to relaxed immigration laws. In 1965, with the Dominican Republic embattled in civil war, the United States invaded Santo Domingo.

Hoping to influence the victory of a pro-American government, U.S. forces monitored elections that saw the victory of Joaquín Balaguer. Thousands of

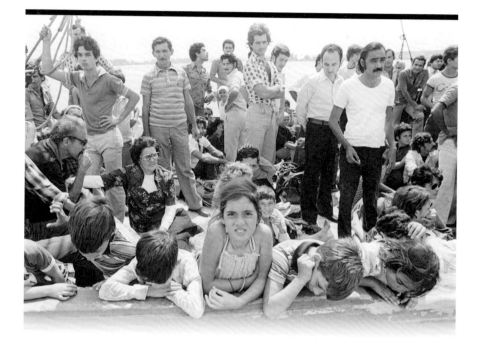

Cuban refugees wait aboard a boat at the port of Mariel, Cuba, bound for Key West, Florida, in 1980. Under pressure from the people, Cuban President Fidel Castro let Cubans leave the Communist island to start a new life in the United States.

Dominicans came to the United States, settling in New York City's Washington Heights neighborhood.

The history of Latinos in the United States, in many respects, has only just begun. As the largest ethnic minority group in the United States, Latinos and Latin-American immigrants will continue to make their mark for years to come.

CHAPTER Four

Civil and Legal Rights

Throughout history, young people have tried to assert their independence and separate themselves from their parents' generation through popular fashion. In the 1940s, *zoot suits* were all the rage for young men. A zoot suit was made up of loosely fitting pants with a high waist and narrow cuffs at the ankles. It was topped with a long jacket with wide, padded shoulders and a long key chain. Thick-soled shoes and wide-brimmed, flat hats often sporting a flashy feather completed the look. This fashion was most popular with African Americans and Chicanos (Mexican Americans). Chicanos sporting this look also became known as *pachucos*. Many people associated this style of dress with gangs and violence, but like teenagers in every era, the pachucos just wanted their own special look and identity.

In 1940s, the pachucos were the targets of attacks known today as the Zoot Suit Riots. In June 1943, a group of sailors and marines on shore leave in Los Angeles claimed that a gang of pachucos attacked them. The following night, a group of over two hundred sailors in uniform stormed into a Mexican-American neighborhood in East Los Angeles. The sailors attacked anyone wearing zoot suits. The servicemen tore off the pachucos' clothing, beat them, and left them in the streets. The assaults occurred for several more nights. Civilians began participating in the assaults as well. The riots spread to other cities in California, Texas, Chicago, and New York. Chicanos were singled out on the streets, pulled from buses, and dragged from movie theaters to be beaten.[1]

The police did not stop the sailors, believing like many in the community, that the beatings would halt an alleged "Mexican crime wave." Hundreds of Mexican-American youths were arrested without cause. The police said that the arrests were "preventive."[2] The Mexican ambassador demanded that the attacks cease. The military police finally stopped these assaults on the fifth night when they forbade the servicemen from going to Los Angeles. However, it was an important lesson for Latinos who realized that they needed to organize politically to protect their civil rights.

Organizing for Change

The oldest Latino organization in the United States is the League of United Latin American Citizens (LULAC). Founded in Texas in 1929, LULAC works for Latinos' rights in education, employment, health, housing, and immigration. In 1954, LULAC took on the state of Texas in the landmark case, *Hernández* v. *the State of Texas*. Up until that time, no one of Mexican origin had ever been called to jury duty in at least seventy counties in Texas. LULAC attorneys took the case to the Supreme Court, winning the right for Mexican Americans to serve on juries. The Supreme Court ruled this exclusion unconstitutional.

The Community Services Organization (CSO) was another organization that fought for Latino civil rights. Founded in 1947, two of its most visible organizers were Fred Ross and César Chávez. Ross and Chávez used effective organizing methods such as the "house meeting" approach.[3] This strategy meant gathering people at a trusted coworker's house where they felt more comfortable. All the people attending would then be asked to host a meeting in their homes so that even more new people could be brought into the movement.

The CSO emphasized voter registration and voter education so that voters could make wise, informed decisions at the polls. By getting more of the workers registered to vote, they could have power over their

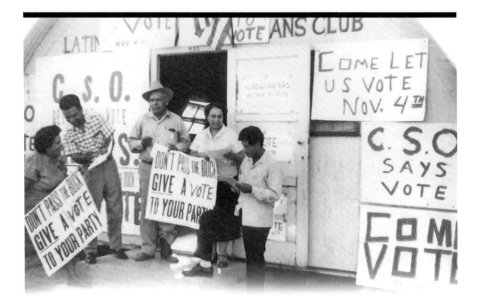

Members of the Community Service Organization encouraged farm workers to vote in elections.

elected officials. Chávez was so effective at getting Mexican Americans registered to vote that he was soon assigned the job of helping Mexican immigrants become United States citizens. In 1959, Chávez became the CSO's executive director in California.

The Mexican American Political Association (MAPA), founded in 1960 in California, strives to represent Hispanics in the political arena. MAPA works toward the social, economic, and civic betterment of all Spanish-speaking Americans through political action. It sponsors community rallies, holds conferences on important issues, and calls for economic boycotts to bring attention to problems faced by Latinos in the United States.

In 1968, the Mexican American Legal Defense and Education Fund (MALDEF) was created. Known as "the legal arm of the Latino community," MALDEF works to foster sound public policies, laws, and programs that protect the rights of Latinos. MALDEF's legal work includes immigration reform, fair voting and citizenship rights, and employment opportunities.

Another organization created during the 1960s was the National Council of La Raza (NCLR). Still very active, this organization focuses on improving opportunities for Latinos by reducing poverty and discrimination. It is a not-for-profit association that is not tied to any political party. NCLR is the largest national Latino civil rights organization in the United States. Its focus on five key areas (assets/investments, civil rights/immigration, education, employment, and health) helps to provide opportunities for individuals and families. NCLR's headquarters is in Washington, D.C., but it is active in forty-one states.

In the political arena, the Raza Unida Party (RUP) was created as an alternative to the traditional two-party system in the United States. Founded in Texas in 1970 by José Angel Gutiérrez and Mario Compean, the RUP's original goal was to improve conditions for Latinos throughout Texas. The party soon spread to other states as well. In September 1972, the party held its first national convention. Meeting in El Paso, Texas, the party's platform included workers' and women's rights, bilingual education, and environmental protection. The party had its share of in-house problems, however, including political disagreements, financial mismanagement, and the arrest of one gubernatorial candidate on drug charges. Eventually, the power and tradition of the two-party system was also too strong and the RUP was disbanded in 1981.

Today, there are many active political organizations that assist Latinos. Mi Familia Vota! (My Family Votes!) is a voter registration project launched by People for the American Way. The project reaches out to unregistered Latinos eligible to vote. Strategies to reach potential voters include going door-to-door, making presentations in community centers, and even setting up information booths in places like supermarkets, barber shops, and cultural festivals. To date, the Mi Familia Vota! project has empowered Latino communities by registering eligible Latino voters.

ASPIRA is perhaps the most well-known program among Latino youth because of its ASPIRA Clubs in schools. Led by Dr. Antonia Pantoja, a group of Puerto Rican professionals established ASPIRA in 1961. By focusing on education and leadership development, they hoped to promote self-esteem and cultural pride. Many of these "aspirantes" went on to become leaders in their communities and helped to train another generation.

Latinos United

In addition to formal organizations, Latinos have also organized at the grassroots level. Individuals and groups of citizens have come together at different times to better the lives of Latinos.

Rodolfo "Corky" Gonzales, a Chicano poet, boxer, and political activist is regarded as one of the early founders of the Chicano Movement, which demanded equal rights for Mexican Americans. In 1968, Gonzales convened the first-ever Chicano youth conference. At the gathering, he unveiled his *Plan Espiritual de Aztlán*. This manifesto (a public declaration of beliefs and policies) demanded that Chicanos be allowed to determine their own political status. Gonzales led demonstrations, boycotts, and student walkouts protesting police brutality, inferior housing, and what he called "the educational neglect of Mexican Americans."[4]

During the Civil Rights movement, students were very involved in politics. One group of Chicano students, the Brown Berets, organized themselves to bring attention to the discrimination that Latinos faced. Many people think of them as the Latino version of the African-American Black Panthers. Originally called the Young Chicanos for Community Action, these high school students decided to wear

Cha Cha Jiménez (left) chairman of the Young Lords, was present at a June 4, 1969 news conference called by the Illinois Black Panther party. Speaking is Bobby Rush, deputy defense minister of the Illinois Black Panther party.

brown berets as a symbol of unity and pride in being brown, rather than black or white. Soon they became known as the "Brown Berets." The Brown Berets were committed to fighting police harassment, unfair educational practices, the lack of political representation, and the Vietnam War.

They became known for leading walkouts, where high school and college students were encouraged to walk out of their classrooms to protest injustice. The group eventually disbanded in 1972.

The Young Lords was another student activist group similar to the Black Panthers. Active in the 1950s and 1960s in Chicago and New York, these young Puerto Rican Americans organized protests and demonstrations to bring public attention to a number of problems. They worked tirelessly on issues such as health care, women's rights, and prisoners' rights. They created a "13-Point Program" that called for things such as liberation for Puerto Rico, equality for women, and an end to racism.[5] The Young Lords were able to set up free breakfasts for schoolchildren, community health tests, clothing drives, and many community events that showed their pride in Puerto Rican culture and history. The group was controversial, however, because it advocated armed self-defense and a socialist society.

One of the issues that the Young Lords focused on was education. The low college acceptance rates for Puerto Ricans and African Americans led to the 1969 sit-in at the south campus of the City University of New York. Students locked themselves in several buildings and forced the school to close down. They asked for an open admissions policy, Black and Puerto Rican studies programs, and Spanish classes for all education majors.

Community members responded by bringing food and blankets to the protesters. There were skirmishes with the police, and after dozens of student activists were arrested, the takeover finally ended. The Young Lords were instrumental in establishing a more open college admissions policy, the creation of Puerto Rican studies programs, and the establishment of several student organizations.

While many of these student groups no longer exist, one student group, MEChA, is still active on college campuses throughout the United States. MEChA (*Movimiento Estudiantil Chicano de Aztlán*; in English, Chicano Student Movement of Aztlán) seeks to promote awareness of Chicano history through education and political action. Founded in 1969, the group's motto quickly became *La Unión Hace La Fuerza* (Unity Creates Strength). MEChA was instrumental in the creation of Chicano studies programs and departments.

The Civil Rights Act

Although many people associate the Civil Rights Act exclusively with African Americans, the law also assisted Hispanic Americans. In 1964, the Civil Rights Act was passed, making it illegal to discriminate on the basis of race, religion, sex, or national origin. Although primarily intended to safeguard the rights of African Americans, the

JFK and The Civil Rights Act of 1964

When President John F. Kennedy addressed the nation on television on June 6, 1963, he said it was time to guarantee equal treatment of every American regardless of color. At the time, much of U.S. society was still segregated (whites and blacks were kept apart). Congress soon began considering legislation that would address voting rights, public facilities, school desegregation, and other due rights.

President John F. Kennedy

Just a few months later, in November 1963, Kennedy was assassinated. Although he was never able to see his vision for a just law become a reality, Kennedy's original proposal resulted in the Civil Rights Act of 1964 just a year later. The Civil Rights Act was signed into law by President Lyndon Johnson on July 2, 1964. The legislation banned segregation in public places such as schools and swimming pools. It also made discrimination in employment and businesses illegal.[6]

Civil Rights Act of 1968

Meant as a follow-up to the Civil Rights Act of 1964, the Civil Rights Act of 1968 outlawed discrimination in housing practices. Also known as Title VIII or as the Fair Housing Act, it prohibits discrimination in the sale, rental, and financing of housing based on race, color, religion, sex, or national origin. Later, the law was expanded to include handicapped individuals and family status. It was signed into law on April 11, 1968, by President Lyndon Johnson just one week after the assassination of Dr. Martin Luther King, Jr.

federal law outlawed all forms of discrimination in employment, public places, and education. It also addressed voting rights and limited the use of literacy tests for the purposes of voter registration.

Although court cases and other laws banning discrimination had been passed before 1964, the Civil Rights Acts included an important provision: No federal funding would be given to any government or organization that discriminated against minorities. This sent a powerful message about the nation's vow of equal opportunity for all citizens.

Latinos Becoming Political Leaders

Latinos are also represented in government at all levels, representing both political parties. The first Hispanic to serve in Congress was Joseph Marion Hernández, elected in 1822 as a delegate to the U.S.

Congress from Florida. The first Latino to serve as a U.S. senator was Octaviano A. Larrazolo, who served in 1928. In 1976, the Congressional Hispanic Caucus (CHC) was created. Started by five Hispanic members of Congress, the CHC sought to ensure that the needs of Hispanics were being met. Today, there are over six thousand Hispanics holding public offices.

When President Bill Clinton was elected, he vowed to have a cabinet that "looked like America." Until that time, presidential cabinets were mostly composed of white men. Under President Reagan, white men made up 85 percent of the appointments. Only one Latino, Secretary of Education Lauro Cavazos, was a member of Reagan's cabinet. Cavazos also served under George H. W. Bush, whose cabinet was 71 percent composed of white men.[7]

President Clinton's presidency was historic in that he appointed three Hispanics to serve on his cabinet. Federico Peña served as secretary of transportation during Clinton's first term and as secretary of energy during the second term. Clinton appointed Henry Cisneros, the former mayor of San Antonio, Texas, as secretary of housing and urban development. Aida Álvarez sat on Clinton's cabinet in her position as the administrator of the small business administration. She was the first Latina and the first Puerto Rican to serve on a presidential cabinet. President Clinton also appointed Bill

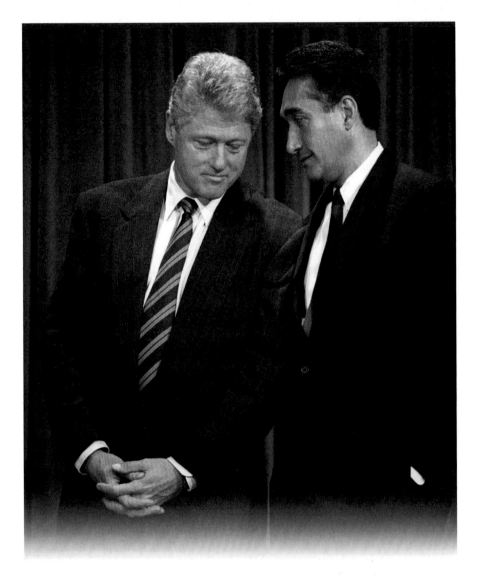

President Bill Clinton listens to Housing Secretary Henry Cisneros in the Old Executive Building in Washington, D.C., in 1994.

Ileana Ros-Lehtinen
(July 15, 1952–)

When Ileana Ros-Lehtinen came from Cuba at the age of seven, little did she know that one day she would become the first Latina and the first Cuban American elected to Congress. This honor came to her in 1982. As a result of her family's experience, the Republican strongly opposes the communist regime in Cuba and works as a human rights advocate throughout the world.

Richardson as the first Hispanic American to serve as the chief U.S. delegate to the United Nations.

George W. Bush appointed two Latinos to his cabinet. Under his presidency, Alberto Gonzales became the first Hispanic to hold the office of attorney general. Bush also appointed Cuban American businessman Carlos Gutiérrez as U.S. secretary of commerce.

Although the lack of Latino governors has been lamented, there have been some notable exceptions. One of the earliest was Romualdo Pacheco who was elected governor of California in 1875. More recently, Bill Richardson was elected governor of New Mexico in 2002. As more and more Latinos become elected officials, the face of the United States's political arena is changing.

Latinos as Voters

The 2004 elections were notable because more Latinos voted at the polls than in any previous election. Approximately 7.5 million Latinos voted, selecting candidates from both the Republican and Democratic parties. With so many Latinos going to the polls, political candidates and officials were openly courting the Latino vote. In response, the National Council of La Raza published a "Voter's Guide" that gave an overview of the issues important to Latinos. Important concerns included access to health care, education, economic opportunities, and immigration.[8]

It is estimated that about 35 percent of Latinos are Republican and 62 percent are Democrats. But, as the National Council of La Raza points out, through elections, Latinos have demonstrated that "they will support strong candidates from both major parties and that they are not tied to a single political ideology."[9] More than ever before, Latinos are involved in the political sphere and are using their votes to improve the quality of life for their communities and families.

Education and Language

In 1945, the Méndez family had recently moved to Westminster, California, in Orange County. Just east of Long Beach and slightly southwest of Anaheim, Gonzalo Méndez and his wife, Felicitas, had leased 40 acres in the small community from a Japanese family. The Japanese family had been sent to one of the ten "relocation centers" established by the U.S. government. During World War II, fear of espionage prompted President Franklin D. Roosevelt to sign Executive Order 9066. The evacuation order resulted in the removal of 120,000 citizens of Japanese heritage from their homes to internment camps for the duration of the war.

There were three children in the Méndez family: Sylvia, Gonzalo, Jr., and Gerónimo. Like their parents, the Méndez children were all U.S. citizens and were completely fluent in English. One of the first things the family needed to do after their move was to register the children in the local school. Because the parents were busy preparing the fields, Gonzalo asked his sister, Soledad Vidaurri, to register the three Méndez children when she went to enroll her own two.

Mrs. Vidaurri had no problem registering her own two children (who did not have a Mexican-sounding last name and were light skinned). But school officials refused to enroll the Méndez children (whose last name was clearly Hispanic and who, unlike their cousins, were dark skinned). The Méndez children were advised to go to Hoover Elementary, "the Mexican school" a few blocks away. For years, the Orange County school system had been segregated on the grounds that Mexican children were "more poorly clothed and mentally inferior to white children."[1]

Infuriated, Gonzalo Méndez contacted attorney David C. Marcus. Marcus had made a name for himself by successfully challenging whites-only public facilities in *López* v. *Seccombe*. Just tried the year before, *López* v. *Seccombe* ensured that all people would have equal access to public pools and parks. Ignacio López, a U.S. citizen who lived in San Bernadino, California, was outraged that he and other Mexican Americans were not allowed to use the public swimming pool. López had served in World

War II and was a graduate of the University of Southern California. Using the Fourteenth Amendment of the U.S. Constitution, Marcus argued that the city had to open public swimming pools to all its citizens. The judge ruled in López's favor and issued a court order.

When Marcus heard the Méndezs' story, he took the case on and filed a lawsuit on the family's behalf on March 2, 1945. The trial took place in July 1945 over the course of two weeks. The actual court order, however, was not delivered until February 1946. The judge ruled that a public school education must be available to all children, regardless of their ethnic origin. *Méndez* v. *Westminster School District et al.* went on to influence the famous Supreme Court case *Brown* v. *The Board of Education of Topeka Kansas*, which outlawed racial segregation in public schools.[2]

Latinos and Schooling in the United States

For Latinos, schooling in the United States has been bittersweet. On the one hand, it has been a way for them to improve financial security for their families and attain the American dream. On the other hand, they have not always been welcome at the schoolhouse door.

Historically, Latino children have been disadvantaged in education for three reasons. First, bilingual education was not offered until the mid-1960s.

Until this time, it was primarily the "sink or swim" method of language instruction that was used. That is, language minority students were placed in a regular classroom with little or no special instruction. Second, migrant farmworkers' status also kept them from receiving a good education. Many school districts refused to educate children because they did not have a permanent residence. Third, because of the high rates of poverty among Hispanics, many Latino children work to help support their families, leading to poor academic achievement and high drop-out rates.[3]

The 2000 census reported that just over 50 percent of Latino students graduate from high school, 9 percent graduate from college, and only 4 percent go on to earn an advanced college degree. By comparison, 84 percent of white students finish high school, 26 percent graduate from college, and 10 percent earn advanced college degrees.[4]

A report issued in 2006 found that of all ethnic groups, Latinos have the highest high school drop-out rate—four times higher than white students and more than double the rate for African-American students.[5] The report warned that failure to graduate from high school was not just bad for Latinos, but the nation as a whole.[6] Research studies have shown that high school dropouts earn about $9,200 less per year than high school graduates. Those who do not

Plyler v. *Doe*

Are children who are born outside the United States and enter the country illegally with their parents allowed to attend American public schools? According to *Plyler* v. *Doe* (1982), yes. In a 5 to 4 decision, the Supreme Court ruled that under the Fourteenth Amendment a state cannot deny school enrollment to children of illegal immigrants. In the majority decision, the Court reasoned that illegal immigrants and their children—although not citizens of the United States—are people "in any ordinary sense of the term" and, therefore, are protected by the Fourteenth Amendment of the U.S. Constitution.

complete high school are also more likely to need government assistance or serve time in prison.[7]

The Chicano Student Walkout

With the Civil Rights Movement sweeping the nation in 1968, thousands of Mexican-American students in East Los Angeles protested poor educational conditions by walking out of five high schools. The students wanted to make a statement about the education that Mexican Americans were receiving. They complained that the schools were overcrowded, that they did not have any Latino teachers, and that there were not enough textbooks to go around. While many of them had college aspirations, most of them were put in vocational classes. They held press conferences and presented written proposals that demanded such things as fixing old buildings, having a more demanding and useful curriculum, and improving the schools' libraries.

The "blowouts" as they were also called, lasted for several days.

At first, the demonstrations were peaceful. But soon the Los Angeles police force was sent out in riot gear. Orders were issued to the police to force the unarmed students back to school. Several students suffered injuries, and community leaders and parents were outraged.

Although in the end the students did not have all their demands met, the walkouts brought attention to the educational inadequacies, and the school board eventually added more academic programs and more Latino teachers were hired.

Years later in 2006, Moctesuma Esparza, one of the students involved in the walkout, unveiled a film he produced about the event. Called *Walkout*, the HBO film was directed by Edward James Olmos. It tells the story of the 1968 walkouts by focusing on Sal Castro, one of the teachers who helped the students organize.

The Bilingual Education Acts

The Bilingual Education Act of 1968 was the first law at the national level that provided extra funding to school districts to meet the special needs of

Spanish-language students. A year after the law was passed, $7.5 million was slated for bilingual education programs. The funds could be used for training teachers to work with language minority students, to develop materials that could be used by English-language learners, and for programs that involved parents in schooling.

But proponents worried that because the Bilingual Education Act was voluntary, it would not be employed as intended. To ensure compliance, amendments to the law were passed in 1974 as a result of a groundbreaking court case in California.

The case was a class action suit against the San Francisco Unified School District. A class action suit is a lawsuit by one or more people on behalf of a large group of people with the same interest or issue. Chinese-American students there protested that they were not receiving an equal education because of their limited English skills. At first, the lower courts ruled that the Chinese students *were* receiving a quality education. But when it reached the Supreme Court, the justices reversed the decision by a unanimous ruling [414 U.S. 563 (1974)]. The justices wrote: "There is no equality of treatment by providing students with the same facilities, textbooks, teachers and curriculum, for students who do not understand English are effectively foreclosed from any meaningful education."[8]

The ruling of the case led to a federal mandate that all school districts take actions to correct educational issues for students whose native language was not English. For Latinos, the landmark decision meant that schools had to ensure that classroom instruction was meaningful for *all* students, including English language learners.

Another important court case was *Castañeda* v. *Pickard* [648 F.2d 989 (5th Cir., 1981)]. This 1981 case involved Mexican-American children in the Raymondville Independent School District in Texas. Parents charged that the teaching practices used in schools violated their children's rights. They argued that the school district did not offer bilingual education programs that helped language minority students. They also charged that because school officials used "ability tracking" to group students, it caused the segregation of Hispanic students.

The Fifth Circuit Court of Appeals agreed with the Mexican-American families. The case established standards for the education of English-language learners, including having qualified staff. This meant that school districts had to hire new staff in some cases and train current staff to make sure they were meeting students' needs.

Educational Challenges

Not all court cases or legislation have been in support of bilingual education. Proposition 227 was passed in 1998 to end bilingual education in California. It was passed by voters by a margin of 61 percent to 39 percent. The law calls for a program to intensively teach children English as soon as they enter school. The law stated:

> Whereas, the English language is the national public language of the United States; and young immigrant children can easily acquire full fluency in a new language if they are heavily exposed to that language . . . It is resolved that: all children in California public schools shall be taught English as rapidly and effectively as possible (Proposition 227, Article I, 1998).

Critics of Proposition 227 said that the law was racist and was anti-bilingual education. They argued that English immersion could be cruel, not effective, and was unrealistic in terms of the time expectations it takes to learn English.

Many also feel that the No Child Left Behind (NCLB) law, passed in 2001, hurts Latino students. By focusing on literacy, NCLB seeks to improve school achievement and hold schools accountable for it. From the onset, the law was controversial because of its emphasis on testing and the threat of withholding federal funding for under-performing schools. But because many Latinos do not do as well on these tests, they are often held back a grade or not allowed to graduate because of poor scores.

Some feel that many of these standardized tests are loaded with bias. Not being fluent in English can

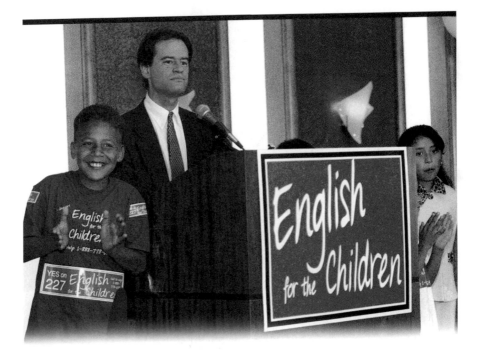

José Antonio González, age ten, (left) applauds with other children as Proposition 227 author Ron Unz addresses the media and proponents of the proposal to end bilingual education in California.

certainly have a negative impact on a student's scores. Not being familiar with American culture and expressions can also result in lower scores.

Educators point out that bias against Latinos is evident in the school curriculum and in textbooks. The curriculum is what students study and when. If students do not see their culture and history reflected in the curriculum, it may result in disinterest and lower academic achievement. Textbooks also need to reflect the many cultures that make up the population. However, school texts do not always do that. Some educational researchers argue that Latinos are regularly omitted from both the school curriculum and from school textbooks.[9]

Affirmative Action

Affirmative action refers to a policy or a program that seeks to eliminate discrimination in education (and employment) against minorities. Many colleges, for example, try to ensure a diverse student body by having special programs to admit ethnic minorities, especially in underrepresented majors or professions.

In 1978, affirmative action was challenged in the case of the *University of California Regents* v. *Allan Bakke*. Bakke was a student trying to gain admission to the medical school at the University of California, Davis. After he was denied entry for the second time, he claimed that he was the victim of "reverse discrimination." He argued that minority candidates were not held to the same entrance standards (GPAs, test scores, etc.) that white students were expected to have. Bakke sued the California university system. The California Supreme Court ruled in Bakke's favor, 8–1. The university system appealed and in 1978 the case was heard before the U.S. Supreme Court.

In their 5–4 decision, the U.S. Supreme Court justices were sharply divided. The court ruled that racial quotas could no longer be used in school admissions. However, the Court did stipulate that race could still be considered in student admissions.

For Latinos, the Bakke decision was devastating. Latino organizations worried that the effect of *Bakke* would be to resegregate American campuses. While most schools did not use the Bakke case to exclude minorities, some did and there have been recent challenges to affirmative action. LULAC has strongly opposed such measures. The LULAC president at the time, Hector Flores said, "LULAC firmly believes that the continuation of affirmative action is a number one priority and is essential to maintaining a diverse student body at our nation's top colleges and universities reflective of the racial and ethnic makeup of our great country, a country of opportunities."[10]

Hopwood v. *University of Texas*

Another important case in the issue of affirmative action is *Hopwood* v. *University of Texas*. In 1992, Cheryl Hopwood was denied admission to the University of Texas Law School. Hopwood, who was white, sued the university maintaining that she was better qualified than some of the minority candidates who had already been admitted. When the trial went to court in 1994, the judge ruled in favor of the university stating that affirmative action programs were still needed because racism was still part of our society.

Hopwood appealed and in 1996, the Fifth Circuit Court overturned the lower court's decision, saying that the university's race-sensitive admission policy could not be used to increase student diversity at the school. The university appealed the decision to the U.S. Supreme Court, though the Court declined to hear the case.

That same year, Proposition 209 was passed in the state of California. Generally seen as an anti-affirmative action law, Proposition 209 prohibited public institutions to use race, ethnicity, or gender in decision making. Public outcry was immediate and a number of organizations, such as the American Civil Liberties Union and the Feminist Majority, issued public statements condemning the measure. Since Proposition 209's passage, there have also been a number of lawsuits challenging it, and its status remains far from settled.

Language Issues

Language is of central concern in many of the controversies surrounding the education of Latinos. For many Latinos, Spanish continues to be the main language spoken in the home. While this fluency in another language can be a source of opportunity, it can also pose challenges in school, at work, and in politics.

The "English-only" movement has affected Latinos in a number of ways.

Twenty-five states have officially declared English to be their official language. For example, in 1986 a referendum was put to the people of California to make English the state's official language. Seventy-three percent of the voters agreed to make English the state's official language.

Many Latinos feel that the English-only movement is an indication of anti-immigrant sentiment. They point out that with each successive generation, immigrants learn English and become absorbed into mainstream American culture. They point out that in Puerto Rico, both Spanish and English are official languages, to no ill effect.

Even though Spanish may not be an official language and it has been challenged aggressively, it remains the second most frequently used language in the United States.

Hope for the Future

Parents and educators realize that succeeding in school and earning high school and college degrees are critical for a good life. To promote educational success, a number of programs have been developed with Latino students in mind.

At the K-12 school level, some magnet and charter schools are targeting Latino students and providing curricular materials that emphasize Latino contributions. Special instruction is also being offered to those students who do not do well on standardized tests. To combat the high drop-out rate for Latino high school students, incentive programs have been established that reward students for good grades and school attendance. As part of the No Child Left Behind Act of 2001, $13.3 billion was earmarked for economically disadvantaged students, many of whom are Latino. These funds are aimed at helping English-language learners become proficient in English, assisting the children of migrant families, and helping to make college education affordable for Latino students.[11]

In 2005, the High School Initiative was launched at the federal level, hoping to combat the high drop-out rate, improve teacher quality, and promote college awareness. The program recognizes the grim educational situation for Latino students. It promises to provide more resources "to those Hispanic students who are most at-risk of dropping out."[12] Critics, however, say that the plan requires more standardized testing and that the funds are coming from budget cuts in other educational areas.

With the average cost of college in the United States nearing twenty thousand dollars per year, one major stumbling block for prospective Latino college students has been the high cost of attending. Many Latino students qualify for financial aid, however. While the Higher Education Act (HEA) was signed into effect in 1965 by President Lyndon B. Johnson, it has lost funding in recent years. This act established the guaranteed student loan program, making financial aid available to all college students who needed it. However, many community leaders charge that the program's budget has been slashed drastically, and not all who qualify receive appropriate aid.

Another obstacle has been lack of knowledge about applying to and attending college. One University of Georgia program, *Vamos a la Universidad* (Let's Go to College), targets bilingual students. Students participate in the program during the summer between the end of middle school and their freshman year in high school. These students have a college mind-set, and many of them will be the first in their families to attend college. *Vamos a la Universidad* tries to simplify the process of applying to, attending, and graduating from college. Program staffer Nadia Madrid reflects on her own background, "We all have different experiences in getting into college. None of my family went to college and I didn't know how to do it."[13]

Also under way is the Development, Relief, and Education for Alien Minors (DREAM) Act. Every year, approximately fifty thousand undocumented students graduate from high school in the United States. But because they do not have legal status, they cannot go to college or trade school because they are not eligible for grants, loans, scholarships, or legal jobs. If this legislation were to be passed, undocumented students could gain resident status and be able to attend an institution of higher education.

Latinos value education and recognize its importance in life success. With the renewed attention that educational issues are receiving, it is hoped that the next generation of Latino students will be the best educated thus far.

CHAPTER Six

Immigration Issues

As Elizabeth Hernández, age twenty-two, left Cuba with her family in the middle of the night, she looked forward to her new life in the United States. After being at sea for three days, they finally spotted land. The rickety boat had reached the Florida Keys on January 4, 2006, just in time. As the boat began falling apart, they reached an abandoned bridge that no longer connected to land. The new bridge, which does connect to dry land, was just 100 yards away.

As the refugees clung to the pilings, they were spotted by the U.S. Coast Guard. The Coast Guard had been instructed to enforce the U.S. policy known as "wet foot/dry foot." Under the controversial practice, refugees who reach U.S. soil are allowed to stay, but those stopped at sea are returned to their native countries.

The U.S. Coast Guard decided that the former bridge was not part of U.S. soil because sections of the bridge were missing and it no longer connected to dry land. Therefore, Coast Guard officials did not think the bridge counted as "dry land." Human rights leaders were outraged, saying that returning the refugees to Cuba was cruel and that they would be persecuted if returned to the island.

Ramón Saúl Sánchez, head of the Cuban-American Democracy Movement went on an eleven-day hunger strike to protest the group's return to Cuba. He and others argued that the Cubans would be treated poorly if they were sent back to their homeland.

On February 28, 2006, a federal judge ruled that the U.S. government had acted illegally when it sent home the fifteen Cubans who had made it to the bridge. Further, the judge ordered federal officials to "use their best efforts" to help the Cubans return to the United States.[1] When Elizabeth Hernández heard the news she said, "I am so happy. I always had hope I would be able to return."[2]

The Controversy Over Immigration

While the United States prides itself on being a nation of immigrants, the issue has been a source of controversy since the beginning of the twentieth century. As millions of immigrants entered the United States through Ellis Island in New York, they

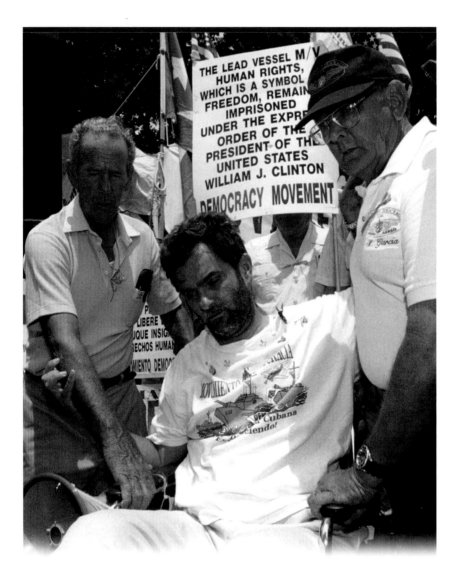

Hunger striker Rámon Saúl Sánchez is helped by supporters, who place him in a wheelchair as they prepare to cross the street to protest in front of a federal building in Miami, Florida, on May 24, 1999.

were met with a mixed reception. On the one hand, they were welcomed for the richness of cultures and the ready pool of labor they brought. On the other hand, they were rejected for their different customs, languages, and jobs they accepted for very low wages.

In 1924, the U.S. Congress passed the Immigration Act of 1924. This act established strict quotas based on country of origin. Immigrants had to apply for visas, pay special fees, and pass certain tests. There was an anti-immigrant feeling in the nation. Through this act the U.S. Border Patrol was also created.

During the Great Depression of the 1930s, most citizens felt the effects of the severe economic decline that was impacting the entire world. In the United States, many people lost their jobs and their homes. As people used up their savings, charities struggled to provide the basic necessities for millions of suddenly poor families. Soup kitchens that made available simple but nutritious meals to the needy were set up in many towns.

For Latinos, the Great Depression was especially devastating. In addition to the economic impact on their families, they also suffered increased prejudice. Although in most cases Latinos had been born and raised in the United States, some Anglos viewed them as foreigners who were taking away much-needed jobs. Mexican Americans in particular were subjected to harassment and intimidation.

Approximately five hundred thousand Mexican Americans were encouraged or forced to leave the country.[3]

But the tide turned after World War II when workers again were in short supply. In 1942, the U.S. government entered into an agreement with the Mexican government to supply temporary workers, known as *braceros*, for agricultural work. Under this program, an estimated 5 million Mexicans were allowed to enter and work in the United States until 1964 when it was discontinued.

On October 3, 1965, President Lyndon B. Johnson signed into law the Immigration and Nationality Act. This legislation ended the national origin immigration quotas that had been in place in the United States since the Immigration Act of 1924. Quotas are set limits or amounts. The elimination of national-origin quotas helped Latino immigrants. However, later legislation has hurt immigration policy for Latinos.

Although the yearly limit of immigrants from any one country is twenty thousand, it is estimated that between 11 million and 12 million people are in the United States illegally. About 7 million of these illegal immigrants are employed in mostly low-level jobs such as construction, food processing, and housekeeping. While some people argue that they are taking away jobs from legal residents of the United States, others argue that without their labor, the U.S. economy could not function.

Although there are quotas as to how many people can emigrate to the United States from a given country, refugees have special consideration. A refugee is a person fleeing persecution in his or her homeland. According to U.S. immigration law, refugees are in a special category that is not subject to immigration quotas. Refugees are granted permission to live and work in the United States and are eligible to receive financial assistance from the government. Examples of refugees are people who have been political prisoners, human rights activists, and people whose religion is discriminated against in their home country. Latin-American refugees include immigrants from Chile, Cuba, Nicaragua, and El Salvador.

In 1986, Congress passed the Simpson-Mazzoli Act. The act specified that anyone who could prove that he or she had been in the country for five years could be granted citizenship. However, fewer people applied for citizenship than expected and many immigrants, especially those from Mexico, continue to live in the United States without permission and without the basic rights of American citizens. The law also stated that American businessmen who knowingly hired illegal aliens could be arrested or fined.

Until 2003, the Immigration and Naturalization Service (INS) was the primary agency in the United States that dealt with immigration issues. Today, the agency is officially called the U.S. Citizenship and Immigration Services (USCIS) and is part of the U.S. Department of Homeland Security.

"Illegal alien" was the term most commonly used for those entering the United States without permission. The term refers to any person who enters and lives in the United States without permission. Because of the term's negative associations, "unauthorized resident" or "undocumented worker" are now more commonly used.

The Border Patrol

In 1924, the U.S. Congress approved the creation of the Border Patrol. The Border Patrol intercepts people trying to enter the United States illegally. From the beginning, the Border Patrol was caught up in controversy.

Today, the Border Patrol uses all kinds of sophisticated methods for its monitoring. Movement sensors, night vision goggles, and helicopters are just some of the equipment they use. The Border Patrol captures about one million people each year at the U.S.-Mexico border. In recent years, the Border Patrol has increased its surveillance along Florida's coasts.

There have also been a number of court cases involving the Border Patrol. One of the more scandalous ones involved high school football coach Benjamin Murillo. Coach Murillo worked at Bowie

High School in El Paso, Texas, a town that is on the Mexico-Texas border. Mexican-American Murillo, who was a U.S. citizen and was wearing a Bowie High School football coaching shirt and shorts, was stopped by the Border Patrol. While one agent pointed a gun to his head, another agent searched his car.

When word spread of the incident, the staff and student body at Bowie High decided to take action. Many of them had also been stopped, questioned, and harassed by Border Patrol agents. Seven of them filed a class action suit, with Coach Murillo serving as the lead plaintiff.

In 1992, the case was decided by a U.S. district court, which found that the Border Patrol had violated the Fourth and Fifth Amendments of the U.S. Constitution. The Fourth Amendment of the Bill of Rights protects people from unreasonable searches. The Fifth Amendment guards citizens' legal rights. The judge said that the high school "provided an oasis of safety and freedom for the students and staff" and that the continued harassment by the El Paso Border Patrol was "both an invasion of their civil rights and the oasis."[4]

As a direct result of the Bowie High School case, the Border Patrol took steps to establish complaint procedures, bilingual complaint forms, and a toll-free telephone number where complaints could be logged. The English-Spanish hot-line number is now displayed on all Border Patrol vehicles.

A Border Patrol agent escorts two girls along a ranch fence after they were found in South Texas brush country north of Laredo, Texas, on June 6, 2006.

The Rio Grande (Spanish for "Big River") provides a natural border between Mexico and Texas and New Mexico. Those who cross the Río Grande are sometimes referred to negatively as "wetbacks." These immigrants often hire people called *coyotes*. Coyotes are paid to smuggle immigrants into the United States.

In 1904, the United States began patrolling the border with Mexico. Large numbers of Mexicans began crossing into the United States during the Mexican Revolution (1910–1917). The conflict caused many Mexicans to flee their homeland in search of safety. As hundreds of thousands of people came to the United States, Congress approved the creation of the Border Patrol in 1924.

By 1953, the Border Patrol had caught more than 865,000 people. The U.S. government felt pressured to stem the flow of immigration. In 1954, Operation Wetback was launched. Although the goal of this campaign was to capture and deport illegal immigrants, it openly focused on Mexicans in general. Close to 4 million people of Mexican heritage were deported.

Some of the illegal immigrants were sent back to their homelands along with their children who had been born in the United States and, by law, were American citizens. Throughout the Southwest, police arrested citizens in raids that targeted Mexican Americans. Some Mexican Americans left the United States on their own as the raids increased.[5]

By many accounts, the immigration officials used a heavy hand in enforcing the law. They questioned any citizen that they thought was "Mexican-looking." Their unfair practices angered many Americans who protested to the government. Operation Wetback was eventually abandoned.

Immigration From Central and South America

Many immigrants from Central and South America seeking a better life attempt to enter the U.S. through Mexico. People from Guatemala, Honduras, El Salvador, and other Latin-American countries resort to the services of the coyotes to help them enter the United States. The human smugglers got their name from their ability to move stealthily at night, evading law enforcement. Coyotes have some defenders, who say that they are a sort of Underground Railroad, helping poor people find jobs and rescuing refugees from persecution. But many others say that the opposite is true and point to the hundreds of deaths the coyotes cause each year.

Because what coyotes are doing is illegal, they take many deadly risks. Every year, hundreds of illegal immigrants die from dehydration, hunger, and heatstroke—often when they are abandoned by coyotes in the middle of a desert. Others die when their overloaded vans and trucks crash, killing those on board.

The number of illegal immigrants, and the abuses they often endure, have led some states, like Arizona, to pass "anti-coyote laws." Under this legislation, those who engage in "human trafficking" are subject to fines and can be jailed. The law is not without critics, however. Some people fear that the immigrants themselves will be prosecuted under this law.

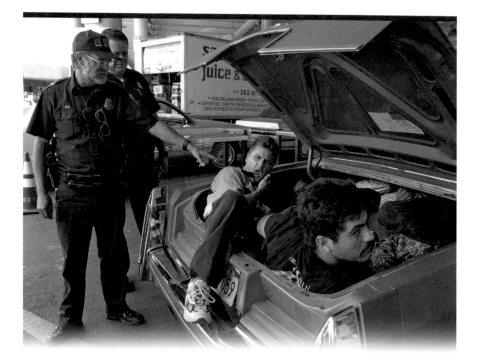

U.S. Customs inspectors open the trunk of a car carrying five suspected illegal immigrants on September 20, 2000, in San Diego, California.

When Arizona's top prosecutor wanted to use the law to charge fifty-one illegal immigrants with a felony, Senator Timothy Bee, who sponsored the legislation, said, "The law was designed to go after those who are involved in drug trafficking and human trafficking for a profit."[6] How the law is applied and enforced continues to be a source of debate and controversy.

Immigration From the Caribbean

For immigrants from the Caribbean, entry to the United States is often by means of watercraft. The crossing is dangerous and many die at sea trying to get to the United States.

Many Dominicans travel to nearby Puerto Rico from where they can take a flight to the United States. Because one does not need a passport to travel from Puerto Rico to the United States, many of them enter the country that way. Tragedy often ensues, however, when Dominicans sail on the channel between the two islands. The relatively narrow 80-mile-wide Mona Passage is rough and shark-filled. Many Dominicans are intercepted by the Border Patrol and returned to their homeland. Others die when their boats capsize.

Puerto Ricans who come to the U.S. mainland are not considered immigrants since they are U.S. citizens. Even though there is a small minority of Puerto Ricans who favor independent status, polls show that the majority prefer continued commonwealth status. The majority points out that this status provides stability.

Cuban immigrants are often given special consideration because of their political status. The Mariel Boatlift of 1980 brought focus to the situation in Cuba and Cuban refugees status in the United States. In 1980, the social and economic climate in Cuba was dismal. To relieve pressure, Cuban leader

The Special Case of Puerto Ricans

While Puerto Ricans are U.S. citizens, many of them choose to emigrate from the island. The "Great Migration" of Puerto Ricans to the United States began right after World War II. Most of these migrants made their way to New York City. Many of them settled in the area known as Spanish Harlem. This population led to the term "Nuyorican," a blending of New York and Puerto Rican. In 1998, New York City mayor Rudolph Giuliani declared June 7 through June 14 as Puerto Rican Week in the city.

Fidel Castro announced he would allow anyone to leave the island nation out of the port of Mariel. Thousands of boats arrived from the United States and anchored in the Cuban port to transport family and friends back to the United States. From April to September when the port was open, 125,000 Cubans fled the island. Many of the boats turned out to be unseaworthy. Twenty-seven people died en route to Florida.

When the Cuban refugees arrived in Miami, authorities were unprepared for the large number of people. Makeshift refugee camps could not meet the demands of the migrants. Although many of them were released soon upon arrival, many others were detained and sent to other processing centers in Pennsylvania, Wisconsin, and Arkansas. As weeks turned into months, many detainees protested, claiming that they were being unfairly held in the camps.

Rumors began to circulate that Castro had loaded the boats with criminals and mental hospital patients. This led to an anti-immigrant sentiment in the United States. Eventually, the Marielitos became part of American society, many of whom have worked to bring other Cubans to the United States.

Immigration Today

One of the more controversial immigration policies has been the Illegal Immigration Reform and Immigrant Responsibility Act of 1996. It is sometimes referred to as "IIRAIRA" for short. Under the law, people could be deported for crimes that had occurred long ago or even for relatively minor offenses, such as shoplifting. The law also gives the right to law enforcement agencies to detain people until they are deported. The law applies even to permanent residents who marry American citizens or who have children born in the United States.

The law was tested in 1998 when Jesús Collado, a permanent resident of the United States, who had lived in New York for twenty-four years, was arrested at Kennedy Airport when returning from his homeland of the Dominican Republic. He was put in jail and told he would be deported back to the Dominican Republic for a misdemeanor crime he had committed in 1974.

Collado's case attracted nationwide attention. During the months that Collado was in jail, he was denied permission to visit his wife and three children, two of whom suffered serious health problems. Supporters argued that the law was unfair and was being applied too harshly. After serving seven months in jail, Judge Douglas B. Schoppert of the New York Immigration Court dismissed the case against Collado and he was released. The U.S. Supreme Court further interpreted the law, concluding that Congress had not intended for IIRAIRA to be applied to people who committed a past crime if that crime would not have been a deportable offense at the time.

After the September 11, 2001 attacks, immigration policy was again under scrutiny. Many felt that foreign-born terrorists were taking advantage of the United States' too-lax immigration policy. While much of the anti-immigrant sentiments were directed at Middle Easterners, Latinos were also condemned.

By 2006, discussion on immigration reached a feverish pitch. As debates regarding immigration raged in Congress, protests, demonstrations, and public meetings focused on the issue. The nation became further divided when *"Nuestro Himno"* (Our Anthem), a Spanish-language recording of "The Star-Spangled Banner" was released on April 28, 2006. It featured singers such as Haitian-born Wyclef Jean, Cuban-American rapper Pitbull,

About one hundred students walked out of classes at Tyler High School in Tyler, Texas, on March 31, 2006, to protest a proposed congressional crackdown on illegal immigrants.

Mexican pop star Gloria Trevi, and Puerto Rican singers Carlos Ponce and Olga Tañón.

Controversy immediately ensued over the Spanish-language version. Critics pointed out that *"Nuestro Himno"* is not an exact translation and that some of the phrases and war references were completely omitted. Charles Key, Francis Scott Key's great-great grandson, charged that the Spanish version is unpatriotic and declared that the national anthem should be sung only in English. He said, "I think it's a despicable thing that someone is going into our society from another country and . . . changing our national anthem."[7] President George W. Bush voiced his discontent with the song saying, "I think people who want to be a citizen of this country ought to learn English and they ought to learn to sing the national anthem in English."[8]

Latinos responded by saying that, as it is with all musical translations, it is impossible to do a literal translation and keep the rhyme and melody intact. Their rendition, they countered, was patriotic and respectful. Adam Kidron, the British music executive who had the original idea for the Spanish-language version, said: "It has the passion, it has the respect, it has all of the things that you really want an anthem to have and it carries the melody."[9]

In May 2006, President George W. Bush announced that six thousand additional Border Patrol officers would be sent to the U.S.-Mexico border to help stop illegal immigrants coming into the United States each year. As part of the same $1.9 billion immigration reform plan, President Bush promised to help legal immigrants attain U.S. citizenship. He said, "We are a nation of laws, and we must enforce our laws. We are also a nation of immigrants, and we must uphold that tradition, which has strengthened our country in so many ways."[10]

By and large, most Latinos support immigration. They point out that the United States is known as a country of immigrants and that this cultural heritage has strengthened the country. Not all Latinos are in favor of immigration, however. Some argue that increased entry of undocumented workers leads to lower wages for everyone. Union leader César Chávez, for example, rallied against illegal immigration by pointing out that undocumented workers are often willing to work for less than the minimum wage. These laborers, desperate for work, would often break the United Farm Workers strikes.

Despite all the controversy associated with immigration, some surveys show that Americans' views of immigrants are less negative today than they have been in the past. Further, those who have contact with immigrants are more positive.[11]

CHAPTER *Seven*

Employment
and Labor

The twelve thousand miners working for John D. Rockefeller's Colorado Fuel and Oil Company were tired of the poor working conditions and wages. It was 1913 and while Rockefeller and other industrialists were getting richer and richer, workers did not seem to be benefiting from company profits. Living and working in Ludlow, Colorado, they were completely dependent on the company store, doctors, and law enforcement.

The United Mine Workers Association began organizing the miners. They presented their demands to the company asking for, among other things, safer working conditions, fairer wages, and the right to choose their own boardinghouses and doctors. When the company refused their demands, the miners decided to strike on September 23, 1913. The strikers were immediately evicted from the company housing and they were forced to set up tents.

At first, the company was able to hire "scabs," non-union replacement workers. But as the striking miners harassed the scabs for working, the company had a hard time keeping employees. Despite the harsh winter, the strikers refused to give in. Company guards were sent to intimidate the strikers. The guards cruised the tent colony with the "Death Special," an armored car mounted with a machine gun. The miners soon dug pits under the tents so that their families could seek shelter from the bullets that were shot indiscriminately at the tents.

On April 20, 1914, the company guards along with state militia, shot at the tents and then burned them down. Twenty people, including two women and eleven children, were killed. Half of those killed were Mexican American. To retaliate, miners in nearby towns rioted, destroying mines and killing mine guards. Only when President Woodrow Wilson intervened and sent the U.S. Army was order restored. Although Rockefeller refused to negotiate an agreement, the event did cause companies to consider using negotiating strategies instead of confrontation.

Years later, folk singer Woody Guthrie immortalized the events in his song "Ludlow Massacre." Although Ludlow is no longer inhabited,

Men and boys at a United Mine Workers strikers' camp in Forbes, Colorado, near Ludlow, eat bread in the snow after their camp was attacked by guards and state militia. Canvas and lumber from tents and luggage can be seen heaped in a pile in the foreground.

a granite monument stands at the site of the massacre. Known as the Ludlow Tent Colony, it is a National Register of Historic Places site. Archaeologists continue to excavate the site and have found tent platforms, cellars, and artifacts related to daily life in the colony as well as from the day of the massacre.[1] The incident is a sobering event in the history of American workers.

Latino Workers in the United States

Latinos have been a part of the U.S. workforce since the very beginnings of the nation. Many of the earliest business owners and laborers worked in the livestock industry. Cattle, sheep, and horses were important parts of the economy in the New World and colonial America.

As the United States expanded into the West, Mexicans were vital in homesteading, cattle driving, and laying down the railways. In the East, Hispanics worked in a number of American cities. Cuban *tabaqueros* (tobacco workers) worked in Key West and Ybor City, Florida, which became known as Cigar City, USA. In Boston's South End, many Puerto Ricans were factory and farmworkers.

By the 1900s, much of the agricultural work in the United States was being done by Mexican migrants. They provided a ready labor force for American agriculture. The Mexican Revolution of 1910 pushed thousands of fearful and desperate Mexicans over the border in search of food and work.

Both world wars stimulated the U.S. economy, and demand for labor grew dramatically. During World War II, the United States was in dire need of agricultural workers. That need resulted in the Emergency Farm Labor Program in 1942, commonly called the Bracero Program. *Brazo* is the Spanish word for arm; a *bracero* is a manual laborer. The Bracero Program was an agreement between the

These Mexicans became bean pickers in Oregon under the Bracero Program in the 1940s.

United States and Mexico that allowed Mexicans to enter the United States for the purpose of working on farms and railroads. An estimated five million Mexicans worked in the United States under this program until 1964 when it was discontinued. While the program provided much needed employment for the Mexican workers, the braceros endured racism as well as difficult living and working conditions. Because the work contracts were in English, the braceros did not fully understand their rights or conditions of employment. When the contracts expired, the braceros were required to return to their homeland. Lee G. Williams, the U.S. Department of Labor official who had been in charge of the program, described it as a system of "legalized slavery."[2]

As the Bracero Program was phased out, another labor program known as *maquiladoras* was started. Maquiladoras are factories in which goods are produced or assembled under a special program that allows the factory owners to pay little or no taxes. Along the U.S.-Mexican border, maquiladoras have been built employing thousands of mostly Mexican female workers. Lured by the prospect of work, hundreds of thousands of Mexicans have immigrated to these border towns. They get paid much lower wages than their U.S. counterparts. Although initially intended to fill the labor need of workers unemployed by the end of the Bracero Program, today most of maquiladora workers are female.

Another program that impacted Latinos was Operation Bootstrap. The English expression of "pulling oneself up by one's own bootstraps" implies that one betters oneself by one's own efforts. It was a program started in Puerto Rico in 1947 that sought to reduce poverty by increasing industry. U.S. companies were lured to the island by low import duties, freedom from taxation, and a desperate workforce. Puerto Rico's economy shifted from agriculture to manufacturing and service industries. At first, it was hailed as an economic miracle. But as time went by, many felt that the only change that the program had brought about was that the formerly poor agricultural workers had merely become poor city workers.

In the 1960s, the plight of migrant farmworkers came to the forefront of the American consciousness. Migrant workers move from place to place depending on which fruits and vegetables are in season and need to be picked. These workers suffer through bad living conditions, low wages, and poor schooling for their children. Many of them do not complain because they are in the United States illegally. They are scared of being deported, or sent back, to their home country.

There is no one better known in the cause for migrant workers than César Chávez. Born in 1927, Chávez founded the United Farm Workers union, which led the struggle to gain basic rights for the workers who harvest the nation's agriculture. Under his leadership, farmworkers successfully negotiated labor contracts with growers for the first time. After his death in 1993, Chávez received the Presidential Freedom Award posthumously from President Bill Clinton in 1994.

Dolores Huerta cofounded the United Farm Workers union with César Chávez. She helped pave the way for other Latinas in this field. Linda Chavez-Thompson, for example, is a Mexican-American union leader who works to improve conditions for workers. She was the first ethnic minority person ever elected to an executive office of the AFL-CIO, the largest federation of labor unions in the country.

Help for Latino Workers

One of the first things Latinos did to help themselves was to set up mutual aid societies. These *mutualistas* help members by pooling resources and then assisting individuals through loans, housing, and help finding jobs. These societies also had a social function in that they helped during births and funerals, and hosted dances and other social events. Mutualistas were especially popular in the first half of the 20th century. With the rising costs of health care in particular, the number of mutualistas has greatly decreased.

Latinos have also organized into workers' unions. Latino workers laboring under unsafe conditions and below minimum wage formed unions to demand changes of their employers. These organized groups have been important in obtaining higher wages, health care benefits, and safer working conditions. Today, about 10 percent of union members are Latino.[3] In 2004, UNITE (Union of Needletrades, Textiles and Industrial Employees) and HERE (Hotel Employees and Restaurant Employees) merged to form UNITE HERE. The organization has close to one million members, many of them Latino.

Dolores Huerta (front left) walks in Merced, California, on August 15, 2002, the first day of a 150-mile march to Sacramento, California, in support of a bill that aimed to help settle farm-labor contract disputes.

Another policy that has helped Latinos in the workforce has been affirmative action. Affirmative action is a series of laws and policies that seeks to stop discrimination for certain groups. It can involve quotas, a certain minimum number of people admitted into a program or hired in a particular job.

Critics, however, say that affirmative action unfairly keeps more qualified applicants out of jobs and disadvantages nonminorities.

The Civil Rights Act of 1964 was also instrumental in helping Latino workers. Title VII of the act was aimed at preventing discrimination on the job. Although initially intended mostly for African Americans, all ethnic groups benefited from the Civil Rights Act.

Latinos in the Work Force

Of all minority groups, Latinos have the highest workforce participation.[4] Yet, Latinos are the second most impoverished group in the United States after American Indians. Part of the reason for this is that Latinos tend to earn less than other workers. When compared to Anglo workers, Latino workers earn 52.6 percent of white workers' salaries. Called the "wage gap," this difference in earning power continues to widen. A recent study found that at all income levels, Latinos tend to make less than whites, African Americans, and Asians.[5] But because of their large numbers, Latino purchasing power has been increasing every year. By 2004, Latino purchasing power climbed to $700 billion per year. It is estimated that it will reach one trillion dollars by 2010.[6]

Latinos also have one of the highest work fatality and injury rates. Latino worker fatalities accounted for 14 percent of the fatal work injuries that occurred

Title VII of the 1964 Civil Rights Act
(National Origin Discrimination)

National origin discrimination means treating people unfavorably because they come from another country or because they do not speak English like a native speaker. Title VII of the Civil Rights Act of 1964 prohibits national origin discrimination in employment. In addition to guaranteeing equal wages and fair hiring and firing practices, the law also safeguards against language discrimination. An employer cannot base a workplace decision on an employee's foreign accent unless the accent interferes with job performance.

in the United States in 2003. This rate is 13 percent higher than the rate recorded for all workers. For foreign-born Latino workers, the rate is even more grim: 69 percent.[7]

Latino in the Business World Today: Prospects and Challenges

There has been a substantial increase in the number of Latino-owned businesses. In 1977, there were about two hundred and nineteen thousand Latino-owned businesses in the United States. Just twenty years later, there were 1.2 million. Even still, Latino-owned businesses make about one hundred and fifty-five thousand dollars per year, as compared to $411,000 made by other businesses in the United

States.[8] While Latino-owned businesses can be found in all states, they tend to survive in states with the largest numbers of Latinos (California, Florida, New York, and Texas).

Most Latino-owned businesses are small, family-run enterprises. Grocery stores, bakeries, record shops, and small restaurants that cater primarily to Spanish-speaking clientele can be found in all barrios in the United States. Where there are large concentrations of Spanish-speaking immigrants, offices that specialize in translation, immigration services, and check cashing can also be found. But increasingly, Anglos are venturing into Latino neighborhoods, making up an increasingly large share of the businesses' customers.

Although Latinos are the fastest-growing group in the United States, they are also the most underrepresented group in corporate offices and boardrooms. Latinos hold only 2 percent of the board seats in Fortune 1,000 corporations. Only one percent of the executive offices at those same companies are occupied by Latinos.[9] Many frustrated Latino executives point to the "glass ceiling" that Latinos have historically encountered in corporate America. "Glass ceiling" refers to an invisible wall that keeps people from being promoted or advancing in a company. Some industries, such as insurance and telecommunications, have hardly any Latinos at all in executive positions. One notable exception is

Hayde Lopez (left) and her husband Salvador Lopez pose in their Miselanea y Video Rodeo shop in Topeka, Kansas. Salvador and his brother own the business, one of a handful of Hispanic businesses in Topeka.

Verizon's Magda Yrizarry, who has been recognized for her commitment to the Latino community.

Despite the dismal statistics, there have been modest gains in corporate America, as more Latinos are joining the executive ranks. Latinas now make up the fastest growing group of business owners and more are becoming top-level managers.[10]

CHAPTER Eight

Latinos Today

The Nuyorican Poets Cafe is located in a small building in New York City's Lower East Side. Passersby might be surprised to learn that inside the humble-looking building some of the most creative Latino poets, actors, and musicians share their work.

Inside, people of all ages and colors sit on bar stools, crouch on the floor, or simply lean against the brick walls covered with posters and artwork. As someone takes to the small stage, a hush comes over the room. For the next few hours, well-known authors as well as amateurs will read their poetry and spark lively discussion.

Called one of "the living treasures of New York" by the Municipal Society of New York, the cafe began around 1973 in the living room of professor and poet Miguel Algarín. With the help of Pedro Pietri and

Pedro Pietri (1944–2004)

Pietri was born in Ponce, Puerto Rico, and moved with his family to the Harlem neighborhood of New York City in 1947. A member of the Young Lords when the group was active, Pietri composed provocative poetry, plays, and artwork, giving voice to many of the hardships Latinos faced. He died of stomach cancer in 2004.

His best known work is the poem "Puerto Rican Obituary." In this poem published in 1973, Pietri recounts the experiences of many Puerto Ricans who migrate to New York in search of the American dream, only to meet discrimination and suffering.

Miguel Piñero, within two years the popularity of the poetry "slams" was so great that a nearby building was rented. Eventually a building was bought in 1980 and the Nuyorican Poets Cafe became a permanent institution. While the cafe may be best known for its plays and poetry slams, it is also a venue for hip-hop, films, and music.[1] It provides a window into Puerto Rican-American culture and history as expressed through the voices of some of America's most renowned Latino artists.

Latino Authors

Latino literature is especially rich and vibrant. From the time of colonization to the present-day United

A mural tribute by artist Chico memorializes poet Pedro Pietri on the façade of the Nuyorican Poets Cafe in New York in 2005.

States, Latinos have been writing about their experiences and developing new forms of creative literature.

Much of Latino literature has had a political bent, describing their injustices and struggles in the United States. Luís Valdéz, a playwright and actor, is widely credited as the founder of the Chicano theater movement. Born to migrant farmworkers, he incorporated much of what he experienced as a child into plays performed by *El Teatro Campesino*

(The Peasants Theater). In 1987 he achieved popular acclaim with his screenplay for *La Bamba*.

Mexican-American Sandra Cisneros addresses many issues specific to Latinas through her writing. Her experiences growing up in Chicago's poor South Side led to her highly praised novel *The House on Mango Street* (1984). In 1995 she received the MacArthur Fellowship "Genius Grant" for her work.

Other Latino authors recount the challenges of immigration. Dominican-American Julia Alvarez published *How the Garcia Girls Lost Their Accents* in 1991. This sensitive story is of four sisters who must adjust to life in America after fleeing from the Dominican Republic. Told through a series of episodes, the story is told in reverse chronology, starting in adulthood and mov-

Sandra Cisneros poses after an interview in New York City in June 1991.

ing backward to their comfortable childhood on the island. Adapting to American life is difficult. It causes embarrassment when friends meet their parents and anger as they are bullied and called "spics." These interconnected stories offer perspectives through Dominican eyes.

El Teatro Campesino
(The Peasants Theater)

Founded in 1965, *El Teatro Campesino* is a theatrical group that reflects the Chicano experience. Founded by Luís Valdéz, El Teatro Campesino was originally started when the United Farm Workers union was on strike for better work conditions. Valdéz wanted to bring entertainment to the workers and encourage the strikers in their hard work.

He approached union leader César Chávez about staging a performance. Valdéz remembers Chávez's reaction: "'There is no money, no actors. Nothing. Just workers on strike.' But he also told me that if I could put something together, it was OK with him. And that was all we needed—a chance. We jumped on top of a truck and started performing. Then something great happened. Our work raised the spirits of everyone on the picket lines and César saw that."[2] Using simple props, masks, and signs, El Teatro Campesino created skits that spoofed the growers and educated people about important issues.

Valdéz also went on to direct films such as *Zoot Suit* and *La Bamba*. His work has been recognized in a number of ways. He is the recipient of the Presidential Medal of the Arts, the Aguila Azteca Award, and the Governor's Award from the California Arts Council.

Cuban-American Oscar Hijuelos was the first Latino to win the Pulitzer prize for fiction. His novel *The Mambo Kings Play Songs of Love* (1989) was so popular it was also made into a movie. The Mambo Kings focuses on two Cuban brothers who immigrate to the United States in the 1950s, during the height of the mambo craze. The brothers' dreams of becoming mambo kings do not go exactly as planned, but the bonds of family and culture are evident throughout the story.

Mexican-American author and poet Gary Soto has written dozens of books for children and young adults. Born in California, his family lived in a working-class barrio in Fresno. These childhood memories form the basis of many of his works. He says, "Even though I write a lot about life in the barrio, I am really writing about the feelings and experiences of most

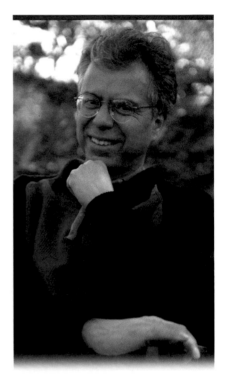

Mexican-American author Gary Soto has written dozens of books.

American kids."[3] His picture books, such as *Too Many Tamales*, give a glimpse into Latino families.

María Irene Fornés is a Cuban-American playwright who has written more than 35 plays, many of them about the lives of Latinas. She has won nine Obie Awards, the highest award for off-Broadway plays. In addition to writing, she helps young Latinos get started in the theater by teaching and mentoring.

Puerto Rican author Esmeralda Santiago has received numerous awards for her writing. Her coming-of-age story, *When I Was Puerto Rican*, is both sad and inspirational. Immigrating to the United States when she was thirteen years old, she went on to attend New York City's Performing Arts High School, Sarah Lawrence College, and Harvard University. Today, Santiago works as a community activist on behalf of the arts and of young people.

Chilean novelist Isabel Allende gained acclaim in the United States with her book *House of the Spirits*. When the novel was made into a movie ten years later, she gained new fans of her work. In addition to the many lectures and book tours she gives throughout the world, Allende is heavily involved in the Isabel Allende Foundation. The foundation helps children and women in need. Through scholarships and grants, the organization furthers education, provides health care, and promotes peace.

Advancing Science and Medicine

Latinos have contributed much to the fields of medicine and science. Since the founding of the nation, Latinos have taken care of the sick, developed new agricultural methods, and invented new machines to improve human life.

In 1959, Dr. Severo Ochoa won the Nobel prize in physiology medicine for his work on the synthesis of RNA (ribonucleic acid), one of the chemical building blocks of life. In 1986, Costa Rican-born Dr. Franklin Chang-Díaz, the first Latino astronaut, went into space. In 1993, Dr. Ellen Ochoa became the first Latina in space when she flew on the shuttle *Discovery*. Also an inventor, Ochoa holds three patents in optical processing.

The chief doctor in the United States is called the surgeon general. In 1990 Antonia Novello was the first Latina—and first woman—to be appointed as the nation's surgeon general. As a child in Puerto Rico, she had a chronic illness of her colon that caused her great discomfort. It was not until she was twenty years old that she was able to get the surgery that would fix her condition.[4] As surgeon general, Novello worked hard to get better health care for children. She also called for special attention to the problems of alcoholism, smoking, AIDS, and violence.

Latinos in the Military

Latinos have fought in every U.S. war, serving their country well and earning honors and awards. During the U.S. Civil War, nearly ten thousand Mexican Americans served in regular or volunteer units. Many Cubans also fought, serving in both the Union and

Ellen Ochoa
Astronaut and Engineer

Ellen Ochoa was valedictorian of her class when she graduated from Grossmont High School in La Mesa, California, in 1975, and again five years later when she earned the baccalaureate degree in physics from San Diego University. With a Stanford engineering fellowship and an IBM pre-doctoral fellowship,

Ellen Ochoa

Ochoa earned a master of science degree in electrical engineering from Stanford University in 1981, and a Ph.D., also in electrical engineering, in 1985.

Ochoa became interested in aviation and applied to the NASA space program. After being rejected at first, Ochoa was finally selected as an astronaut from close to two thousand applicants. In 1990, she became the first Latina selected for the space shuttle program. And when the space shuttle *Discovery* roared into space in April 1993, Ochoa became the first Latina to travel into space.

Confederate armies. In the Spanish-American War, a large number of Latinos, primarily Mexican Americans, served to end the war with Spain. In 1917, just before the United States entered World War I, Puerto Ricans were granted U.S. citizenship and became eligible for military service. Subsequently, 18,000 Puerto Ricans served in the war.

During World War II, more than four hundred thousand Latinos served the U.S. Armed Forces, more than any other ethnic group. At least sixty-five thousand were Puerto Rican, including two hundred *puertoriqueñas* who served in the Women's Army Corps. When these veterans returned from the war, they used their G.I. benefits to further their education and buy homes. Twelve Latinos earned the Medal of Honor during World War II.

Latinos also distinguished themselves in a number of ways in the Korean War. The Borinqueneers, the 65th Regimental Combat Team from Puerto Rico, earned their commander's highest praise when he wrote *Puerto Rico's Fighting 65th U.S. Infantry: From San Juan to Chorwau*. General William Harris wrote, "No ethnic group has greater pride in itself and its heritage than the Puerto Rican people. Nor have I encountered any that can be more dedicated and zealous in its support of the democratic principles for which the United States stands. Many Puerto Ricans have fought to the death to uphold them."[5] During the Vietnam conflict, eighty thousand

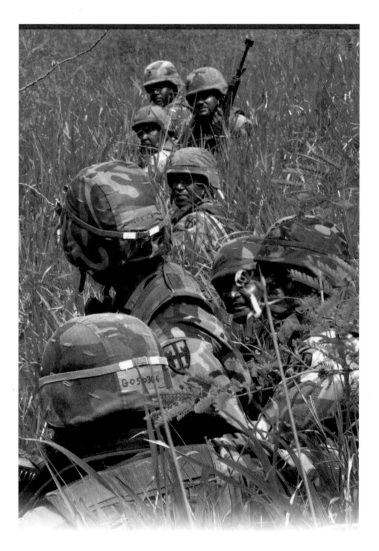

U.S. Army soldiers from the 130th Engineering Battalion of the Puerto Rico National Guard take cover in a grassy area during Convoy Ambush Training at the Leadership Reaction Course at Camp Santiago in Salinas, Puerto Rico.

Latinos served in the Armed Forces. And during the Persian Gulf War of 1990–1991, close to twenty-five thousand Latino men and women served in the operations Desert Shield and Desert Storm.

Currently, there are more than eighty-five thousand Latinos on active duty. These numbers are expected to grow as all three branches of the Armed Forces increase their recruitment of Latinos. And at all the U.S. military academies, the percentage of Latino students is on the rise. To date, forty Hispanic Americans have earned the Congressional Medal of Honor, the nation's highest military award.

Latino Athletes and Sports Heroes

Latinos have long contributed to sports in this nation. In 1871, Esteban Bellan was the first Latino to play major-league baseball. Since then, Latinos have excelled in American baseball. Roberto Clemente, one of baseball's greatest players of all time, won twelve Gold Glove Awards and was the first Puerto Rican to be voted Most Valuable Player. He was a great humanitarian as well. Born in Puerto Rico in 1934, he worked tirelessly to improve the condition of the poor in his homeland. He died in a plane crash in 1972, en route to take badly needed supplies to earthquake victims in Nicaragua. He was elected to the Baseball Hall of Fame in 1973.

Dominican-American Alex Rodriguez has received many awards for his excellent playing as a shortstop. In that position, he holds the record for most home runs in a single season. He was named the 2003 Most Valuable Player in the American League. Called A-Rod by his many fans, Rodriguez is also known for his charitable giving. In 2002, Mark Light Stadium in Miami, Florida, was renamed Alex Rodriguez Park after he donated $3.9 million to renovate the facility. He also established a Boys and Girls Club and donated two hundred thousand dollars to a children's mental health center in Washington Heights, New York.

In 1972, when this photo was taken, Roberto Clemente was playing for the Pittsburgh Pirates.

Great Latino names in professional golf include Lee Trevino, Chi Chi Rodriguez, and Nancy Lopez. Puerto Rican Chi Chi Rodriguez was inducted into PGA's World Golf Hall of Fame in 1992. Mexican-American Lee Trevino was 1971's PGA Player of Year.

Mexican-American professional golfer Nancy Lopez is widely regarded as one of the greatest women golfers of all time. She began to play golf when she was eight years old and was only twelve years old when she won the New Mexico Women's Amateur tournament. Winning forty-eight titles, she is one of the top pro golf money winners of all time. She was inducted into the LPGA's World Golf Hall of Fame in 1989.

There are now many Latinos on the professional tennis circuit. Argentinian-American Gabriela Sabatini was the U.S. Open singles champion in 1990. Dominican-American Mary Jo Fernandez was on the U.S. Olympic Team in 1992 and 1996, and won a gold medal in 1992.

Latinos in the Entertainment Industry

Since the beginning of the history of Hollywood films, during the silent film age, Latinos have been entertaining the country. Hispanic actresses like Myrtle González, Dolores del Río, and Beatriz Michelena were popular silent film stars. Many of these film stars made the transition to "talkies" in the 1920s and 1930s. Films in subsequent decades featured actors such as Fernando Lamas, Anthony Quinn, Rita Hayworth, José Ferrer, Ricardo Montalbán, Chita Rivera, and Rita Moreno.

Perhaps the most well known of all Cuban entertainers was Desi Arnaz. Born to wealthy parents in Santiago de Cuba, Arnaz and his family fled to the United States after a revolution in 1933 left them in peril. By the late 1930s, he was well-known in the United States as a bandleader, musician, and singer. But it was when he married

Lucille Ball and costarred with her on *I Love Lucy* that he earned worldwide acclaim. As a producer, he pioneered the "three camera" technique, live studio audiences, and was the first to use film to preserve TV shows for reruns. *I Love Lucy* continues to be one of the most treasured shows of all time.

Puerto Rican actor Raúl Juliá made a name for himself in movies such as *Kiss of the Spider Woman* and *The Addams Family*. Before that, New York audiences appreciated his roles in Shakespearean plays and Broadway musicals. He was also well known for his humanitarian efforts, especially his desire to end hunger.

Today, Latino stars include Martin Sheen (and his sons Charlie Sheen and Emilio Estévez), Andy Garcia, Edward James Olmos, Rosie Pérez, Jennifer López, Marc Anthony, and Jimmy Smits.

Latinos in Music

The 1940s and 1950s saw the emergence of dance crazes from Latin America. Music and dances known as the rumba, mambo, and chachachá overtook the nation during this time. Based on Afro-Cuban percussion and beats, they formed the basis for later Latin music.

Latinos also made an impact on the rock and roll scene. Ritchie Valens, best known for his hit songs "Donna" and "La Bamba," was born Richard Valenzuela in Los Angeles in 1941. His song "La

Rita Moreno
(December 11, 1931–)

Rita Moreno is only one of two artists who have won all four major entertainment awards (the Oscar for films, the Emmy for television, the Tony for theater, and the Grammy for music). Born Rosa Dolores Alverio in Humacao, Puerto Rico, she moved to New York City at the age of five. She soon began a career in acting, often singing and dancing as well. She is best known for her performance as Anita in the film *West Side Story* and as a regular cast member on TV's *The Electric Company*. In June 2004, she received the Presidential Medal of Freedom from President George W. Bush for her contributions to American culture.

Bamba" was a rock and roll version of a traditional Mexican song. Valens's life was later chronicled in the 1987 movie *La Bamba*. The Mexican-American group Los Lobos rerecorded the hit title song for the movie and a whole new generation discovered his music.

Salsa music (in Spanish, "salsa" refers to a spicy sauce) became very popular in the 1960s and 1970s. Through the work of musicians such as Tito Puente, Willie Colón, Johnny Pacheo, Ray Burretto, Eddie Palmieri, Héctor Lavoe, Celia Cruz, and Rubén Blades, American audiences began to appreciate the multiple sounds and beats this genre could include.

Rubén Blades

After moving from Panama to the United States and becoming aware of social issues and injustices in the world, Rubén Blades began to develop his own singing style and wrote salsa songs with a message. Blades is widely credited as being the first salsa singer to write his own songs, and the first to include politics in his music. He was instrumental in developing one of the varieties of salsa known as *salsa conciente*.

Rubén Blades performs at Caracas, Venezuela's University Stadium in January 2001.

One music reviewer feels that the main message in Blades's songs is "to stimulate thought, to raise consciousness."[7] Another journalist wrote that the singer's songs "are not of partying, but of protest."[8]

Blades started a new political party in his homeland and ran for the presidency of Panama. Although he did not win, several party representatives were elected to government positions.

Simultaneously, the Latin sounds of Carlos Santana and his band also helped to popularize Latino music.

Merengüe is another type of popular Latino music. Lively and joyful, it is music that is usually danced to. While its origins are disputed, merengüe can be traced to the second half of 18th century. Merengüe, as a music and dance form, is most strongly identified with the Dominican Republic.

In the pop music world, Cuban-American Gloria Estefan brought Latin rhythms to Top 20 songs. As both a singer and musician, Estefan became a beloved performer with hits such as "Conga," "Dr. Beat," and "Rhythm is Gonna Get You."

Reggaeton is also enjoying popularity in the United States. Originating in Panama with reggae beats, reggaeton is a form of dance music very popular with Latino youth. The music is a blend of Jamaican reggae with traditional Latin-American beats and rhythms. It is often sung in Spanglish, a mixture of Spanish and English.

Latinos in U.S. Popular Culture

American popular culture is heavily influenced by Latino cultures. Many popular "American" foods have their origins in Latino culture. Foods such as tortillas, nachos, and flan have become commonplace in the United States. Pop and hip-hop music often have Latin rhythms or even Spanish words in the lyrics.

Today, the influence of Spanish can be seen in a number of ways in American English. Many cities in the Southwest such as Los Angeles, Santa Fe, and San Diego are all testaments to their Hispanic origins. Common "American" words such as *rodeo*, *mosquito*, *cargo*, and *patio* all have their origins in the Spanish language.

Spanish-language newspapers and radio and television stations are the norm in many U.S. cities. Daily newspapers such as *Noticias del Mundo* in Los Angeles, *El Nuevo Herald* in Miami, and *El Diario* in New York all serve to keep their readers informed about current events and reinforce their cultures.

In addition to dozens of local Spanish-language stations, Latinos also enjoy several television stations that broadcast nationally. Telemundo and Univision are two companies that offer Spanish-speaking TV programming that includes sports, news, variety shows, and soap operas.

Latinos in Government

Since 1960, more Latinos have been elected to Congress than in the previous 140 years.[9] Even still, only 3 percent of the members of Congress and 5 percent of the representatives in the House are Latino. Most of these government leaders are members of the Congressional Hispanic Caucus, an influential group of lawmakers.

Latinos Today

Since it was first established in 1976, the Congressional Hispanic Caucus has been trying to improve conditions for Latinos in the United States. It was organized by five Latino Congress members who recognized the special needs of Latinos. The CHC promotes issues such as better health care, bilingual education, and workers' rights.

One member of the CHC, Rubén Hinojosa, is a Representative from Texas. As the son of poor Mexican immigrants, he learned from his parents early on that education was the way to a better life. As the head of the Subcommittee on Higher Education, he works hard to improve Latinos' access to a college education. He points out that while more Latinos are graduating from high school and going to college, there is still much work to be done. Hinojosa believes that many low-income students are qualified to go to college but cannot due to financial barriers. As a result, he argues, many talented people are not developing their full ability.[10]

The CHC was instrumental in getting the passage of HR 2134 in the House of Representatives on September 27, 2006. With this legislation, a commission would have been appointed to recommend a plan of action for the creation of a National Museum of the American Latino. As part of the Smithsonian Museum complex, this effort would have documented Latino history and culture. Unfortunately, the bill was never passed in the

Senate and did not become law. Supporters hope that it will be reintroduced in the future.

Latinos are an important part of the social fabric of the United States. They have played a vital role in many ways. While their history and contributions to the United States are undeniable, Latinos continue to work hard to be a part of American society. Although gains have been made in education, employment, and civil rights, Latinos still face prejudice and discrimination. The new generation of Latinos are picking up where previous generations have left off.

Timeline

1492	Columbus embarks on his historic exploratory trip.
1513	Juan Ponce de León explores *La Florida*.
1565	St. Augustine, the oldest city in the United States, is established by the Spanish in Florida.
1769	Father Junípero Serra establishes a mission in San Diego, California.
1848	Mexican-American War is brought to an end with the Treaty of Guadalupe Hidalgo.
1898	Puerto Rico and Cuba are ceded by Spain through its defeat in the Spanish-American War.
1910	Seeking safety from the Mexican Revolution, thousands of Mexicans immigrate to the Southwest.
1917	Jones Act is passed, granting all Puerto Ricans U.S. citizenship.
1924	Immigration is curtailed and the Border Patrol is founded through an act of Congress.
1942	Start of the Bracero Program, an agreement between the U.S. and Mexican governments to bring temporary agricultural workers, known as braceros, to the United States.
1943	Zoot Suit Riots occur.

1947	Operation Bootstrap begins in Puerto Rico.
1954	Operation Wetback is launched to capture and deport illegal immigrants.
1959	Fidel Castro wins a revolution in Cuba, causing thousands to flee to the United States.
1962	César Chávez and his associates found the National Farm Workers Association.
1964	Civil Rights Act is passed.
1966	César Chávez leads a 340-mile march to bring attention to farm workers' poor living and working conditions. Soon after, the United Farm Workers union is formed.
1970	La Raza Unida Party is founded.
1973	Nuyorican Poets Cafe is founded in New York City.
1978	Affirmative action is challenged in the case of the *University of California Regents* v. *Allan Bakke*.
1980	The Mariel boatlift brings 125,000 Cuban refugees to the United States.
2006	President George W. Bush assigns an additional 6,000 Border Patrol officers to the U.S.-Mexico border; *Nuestro Himno* debuts.

CHAPTER Notes

CHAPTER 1. Fighting for Rights

1 | Susan Ferriss and Ricardo Sandoval, *The Fight in the Fields* (New York: Harcourt Brace, 1997), p. 119.

2 | Jacques E. Levy, *Cesar Chavez: Autobiography of La Causa* (New York: Norton, 1975), p. 246.

CHAPTER 2. Who Are the Latinos?

1 | "2005 American Community Survey," *U.S. Census Bureau*, <http://factfinder.census.gov> (February 13, 2007).

2 | "Rodolfo Gonzales, advocate for 'Chicano power,' 76," *The Boston Globe online*, April 15, 2005, <http://www.boston.com/news/globe/obituaries/articles/2005/04/15/rodolfo_gonzales_advocate_for_chicano_power_76> (April 26, 2006).

3 | "Hispanic Population of the United States, Current Population Survey: Definition and Background," *U.S. Census Bureau*, <http://www.census.gov/population/www/socdemo/hispanic/hispdef.html> (February 16, 2006).

4 | "Hispanic Population," *U.S. Census Bureau*, <http://www.census.gov/PressRelease/www/releases/archives/facts_for_features_special_editions/007173.html> (August 15, 2006).

CHAPTER 3. Coming to America

1 | James A. Lewis, "Las Damas de la Havana, el Precursor, and Francisco de Saavedra," *The Americas*, Vol. 37, No. 1 July, 1980, pp. 83–99.

2 | "The Félix Longoria Affair," *Hispanic Online*, <http://www.hispaniconline.com/hh02/history_heritage_sidebar_felix_longoria.html> (June 15, 2006).

3 "Pedro Pan," *All Things Considered, National Public Radio*, May 3, 2000, <http://www.npr.org/templates/story/story.php?storyId=1073679> (June 29, 2006).

4 Yvonne Conde, *Operation Pedro Pan: The Untold Exodus of 14,048 Cuban Children* (New York: Routledge, 1999), p. xiii.

CHAPTER 4. Civil and Legal Rights

1 George Ochoa, *The New York Public Library Amazing Hispanic American History* (New York: John Wiley and Sons, 1998), p. 71.

2 Rodolfo Acuña, *Occupied America* (New York: Longman, 2000), p. 272.

3 Dolores Huerta, "Reflection on the UFW Experience," July/August, *Center Magazine*, vol. 18, 1985, p. 2.

4 "Rodolfo Gonzales, advocate for 'Chicano power,' 76," *The Boston Globe online*, April 15, 2006, <http://www.boston.com/news/globe/obituaries/articles/2005/04/15/rodolfo_gonzales_advocate_for_chicano_power_76> (April 26, 2006).

5 *The Sixties Project*, <http://lists.village.virginia.edu/sixties/HTML_docs/Resources/Primary/Manifestos/Young_Lords_platform.html> (May 4, 2006).

6 "Civil Rights Act (1964)," *Our Documents.gov*, <http://www.ourdocuments.gov> (August 15, 2006).

7 Susan Page, "Bush is opening doors with a diverse Cabinet," *USA Today*, December 9, 2004, <http://www.usatoday.com/news/washington/2004-12-09-diverse-usat_x.htm> (December 2006).

8 *NCLR Voter Guide* (Washington, D.C.: NCLR 2006).

9 Ibid., p. 1.

CHAPTER 5. Education and Language

1 Frederick P. Aguirre, "*Mendez* v. *Westminster School District*: How It Affected *Brown* v. *Board of Education*," *Journal of Hispanic Higher Education*, Vol. 4, No. 4, October 2005, pp. 321–332.

2 Ibid., p. 322.

3 Carter Smith and David Lindroth, *Hispanic-American Experience on File.* (New York: Facts on File, Inc., 1999), p. 6.18.

4 "People: Education," *U.S. Census Bureau,* <http://fact finder.census.gov/jsp/saff/SAFFInfo.jsp?_pageId=tp5_education> (August 17, 2006).

5 "President's New High School Initiative, Other Proposed Programs Tackle Issues Important to Hispanics," *U.S. Department of Education*, February 23, 2005, <http://www.ed.gov/news/pressreleases/2005/02/02232005a.html> (August 18, 2006).

6 Haya El Nasser, "Report: Hispanics Lagging in Education," *USA Today*, March 2, 2006, p. 3A.

7 Amanda Paulson, "Dropout Rates High but Fixes Under Way," *Christian Science Monitor*, March 3, 2006, p. 1.

8 *Lau* v. *Nichols*, 414 U.S. 563, CERTIORARI TO THE UNITED STATES COURT OF APPEALS FOR THE NINTH CIRCUIT, No. 72-6520, argued December 10, 1973, decided January 21, 1974, <http://www.law.cornell.edu/supct/html/historics/USSC_CR_0414_0563_ZS.html> (June 29, 2006).

9 Christine E. Sleeter and Carl A. Grant, "Race, Class, Gender, and Disability in Current Textbooks," in Michael W. Apple and Linda K. Christian-Smith, Eds., *The Politics of the Textbook.* New York: Routledge, pp. 78–110.

10 "Affirmative Action Critical to Latino Advancement," *LULAC.org*, <http://www.lulac.org/advocacy/press/2003/affirmaction.html> (August 21, 2006).

11 Adam Chavarria, *Hispanic Outlook in Higher Education*, June 20, 2005 (Vol. 25, No. 19), p. 12.

12 "President's New High School Initiative, Other Proposed Programs Tackle Issues Important to Hispanics," *U.S. Department of Education*, February 23, 2005, <http://www.ed.gov/news/pressreleases/2005/02/02232005a.html> (August 18, 2006).

13 | Chris Reinolds, "Bilingual Summer Camp for Gifted Pupils," *The Atlanta Journal-Constitution*, August 10, 2006, p. 14JF.

CHAPTER 6. Immigration Issues

1 | "Judge says rejecting 15 Cubans was wrong," *St. Pete Times*, March 1, 2006, p. 5B.

2 | Laura Wides-Muñoz, "Judge Rules in Favor of Cubans on Bridge," February 28, 2006, <http://thecomplete story.blogspot.com/2006/02/judge-rules-in-favor-of-cubans-on.html> June 13, 2006.

3 | George Ochoa, *The New York Public Library Amazing Hispanic American History* (New York: John Wiley and Sons, 1998), p. 69.

4 | *Murillo et al.* v. *Musegades*, 809 F. Supp. 487 (W.D. Texas 1992), LexusNexus Academic Index, August 17, 2006.

5 | PBS, "The Border: Operation Wetback," <http://www. pbs.org/kpbs/theborder/history> (June 13, 2006).

6 | Amanda Lee Myers, "Lawmakers Say Prosecutor Misinterpreting Immigration Law," *The Associated Press,* March 4, 2006, August 15, 2006 from LexisNexis.

7 | "Spanish 'Star Spangled Banner'—Touting the American Dream or Offensive Rewrite?" *ABC News*, April 27, 2006, <http://www.abcnews.go.com/WNT/story?id=1898460> (May 2, 2006).

8 | "The Anthem Ought to Be Sung in English," *St Petersburg Times*, April 29, 2006, p. 12A.

9 | ABC News, "Spanish 'Star Spangled Banner'—Touting the American Dream or Offensive Rewrite?" April 27, 2006, <http://www.abcnews.go.com/WNT/story?id=1898460> (May 2, 2006).

10 | Anita Kumar, "Bush Sending Guard to Border," *St. Pete Times*, May 16, 2006, p. 1A, 4A.

11 | "Immigration in America," *National Public Radio*, October 6, 2004, <http://www.npr.org/news/specials/polls/2004/immigration> (June 13, 2006).

Chapter Notes

CHAPTER 7. Employment and Labor

1   *University of Denver*, <http://www.du.edu/anthro/ludlow.html> (March 2, 2006).

2   "The Bracero Program," *The Farm Workers Web Site*, <http://www.farmworkers.org/bracerop.html> (February 16, 2006).

3   "Union Members Summary 2005," *U.S. Department of Labor*, <http://www.bls.gov/news.release/union2.nr0.htm> (June 20, 2006).

4   *U.S. Department of Labor, Bureau of Labor Statistics*, <http://www.bls.gov/opub/working/page4b.htm> (June 20, 2006).

5   Michael De Give, "Wage Gap Widens for Hispanic Workers," *Santa Cruz Sentinel*, September 2, 2002, <http://www.santacruzsentinel.com/archive/2002/September/02/local/stories/01local.htm> (June 20, 2006).

6   "Hispanic Purchasing Power Surges to $700 Billion," *HispanicBusiness.com*, May 2004, <http://www.hispanicbusiness.com/news/newsbyid.asp?fpa=0&id=16041> (June 20, 2006).

7   *U.S. Department of Labor*, <http://www.bls.gov/iif/peoplebox.htm> (June 15, 2006).

8   Sonia G. Benson ed., *The Hispanic American Almanac* (New York: Gale, 2003), p. 341.

9   Julie Bennett, "Boosting the Hispanic Ranks of Corporate America," *CareerJournal.com*, <http://www.careerjournal.com/myc/diversity/20030321-bennett.html> (February 28, 2007).

10   Benson, pp. 343–344.

CHAPTER 8. Latinos Today

1   *Nuyorican Poet's Café*, <http://www.nuyorican.org> (June 22, 2006).

2   Max Benavidez, "Cesar Chavez Nurtured Seeds of Art," *Los Angeles Times*, April 28, 1993, p. 1.

3   "Gary Soto Biography," <http://www.notablebiographies. com/news/Sh-Z/Soto-Gary.html> (June 22, 2006).

4   Antonia Novello, M.D., <http://www.achievement.org/ autodoc/page/nov0bio-1> (June 22, 2006).

5   "On the Battlefront," *Hispanic Online*, <http://www. hispaniconline.com/hh02/history_heritage_on_the_ battlefront.html> (June 15, 2006).

6   "The Eugene A. Obregon/Latino Medal of Honor Campaign," <http://www.azteca.net/~cmhlatino/ corrido> (June 29, 2006).

7   Achy Obejas, "Rubén Blades Gives New Meaning to *Salsa*," *Nuestro*, April 1984, p. 51.

8   Anthony DePalma, "Rubén Blades: Up From Salsa," *New York Times Biographical Service*, vol. 18, no. 6, June 1987, p. 595.

9   "Hispanic Americans in Congress, 1822–1995," *The Library of Congress*, <http://www.loc.gov/rr/hispanic/ congress/introduction.html> (February 28, 2007).

10   "The House's New Face on Higher Ed," *Inside Higher Ed*, <http://www.insidehighered.com/news/2007/02/16/ hinojosa> (February 26, 2007).

Glossary

barrio—Neighborhood or section of a city in which Latinos live.

boycott—Not buying a particular product as a means of protest.

bracero—Manual laborer.

Chicano/Chicana—A person of Mexican descent originating from the Spanish word "Mexicano." While it was at first considered an insult, by the 1960s, Mexican-American activists began using the term with pride.

coyotes—People who help smuggle immigrants into the United States.

criollos—People born in the New World of Spanish descent.

Hispanic—Someone whose family comes from Spanish-speaking countries in Latin America; considered by some, who prefer the term "Latino," to have too much stress on European roots.

Latino/Latina—Someone whose family comes from Spanish-speaking countries in Latin America; often used interchangeably with "Hispanic" although some favor "Latino" because it puts more emphasis on Latin-American origins.

La Raza—Spanish for "the race." The term was popularly used in the 1960s by Mexican-American political activists. Today the term is used by other Hispanic Americans as well.

maquiladora—Factory along the U.S.-Mexico border where goods are produced under a program that allows owners to pay little or no taxes.

marielitos—Cubans who emigrated to the United States on the Mariel Boatlift in 1980.

mestizo—A person of mixed American Indian and Spanish ancestry.

mulatto—A person of mixed African and European ancestry.

mutualistas—Mutual aid societies.

refugee—A person fleeing persecution in his or her homeland.

strike—The stopping of work by employees to demand of their employers better conditions and/or higher wages.

wetback—A derogatory term for those immigrants, usually Mexican, who cross the Río Grande into the United States.

Further Reading

Books

Atkins, S. Beth. *Voices from the Fields: Children of Migrant Farm Workers Tell Their Stories.* New York: Little, Brown, 2000.

Kent, Deborah. *The Changing Face of America: Hispanic Roots, Hispanic Pride.* Chanhassen, Minn.: The Child's World, 2004.

Mintzer, Richard. *Latino Americans in Sports, Film, Music, and Government: Trailblazers.* Philadelphia: Mason Crest Publishers, 2006.

Powell, John. *Encyclopedia of North American Immigration.* New York: Facts on File, Inc., 2005.

Schwartz, Eric. *Latino Economies in the United States: Job Diversity.* Philadelphia: Mason Crest Publishers, 2005.

Stavans, Ilan. *Latino USA: A Cartoon History.* New York: Basic Books, 2000.

Internet Addresses

Famous Hispanics in the World and History
<http://coloquio.com/famosos/alpha.htm>

Library of Congress HLAS Online: Handbook of Latin American Studies
<http://memory.loc.gov/hlas/>

Index